IMAGES
of America

RICHMOND HEIGHTS
1868–1940

In Memory of Evelyn Dellene Grant
1937–1999

Without Evelyn's tireless efforts to preserve the history of Richmond Heights, there would be no archives and no historical society. Her position as department secretary for the Richmond Heights Building Department from 1974 to 1994 enabled her to be in contact with many people and discover potential archival materials. She began collecting photographs and artifacts, saving newspaper and journal articles, and storing these items first at city hall and then in her home when the archives became too large. In 1982, Evelyn worked with attorney Richard Ulrich to incorporate the Richmond Heights Historical Society and form a board of directors. As the historical society's first president, she organized regular board and membership meetings, set up historical displays, and continued to amass personal histories, photographs, and artifacts to enlarge the collection.

Evelyn married Paul Grant in 1955, and two years later they moved to their home on Williams Avenue in Richmond Heights, where they raised three children: David, Steven, and Paula. All the Grant children attended school in the Maplewood-Richmond Heights District. Evelyn was active in the Chaney Parent-Teacher Association, the Lyndover Junior High Mothers' Club, and the Maplewood-Richmond Heights High School Mothers' Club. Elected to the district's school board, she served as the board's director, president, and vice-president. She was appointed by former mayor Richard Provaznik to represent the city on the University of Missouri's St. Louis County Extension Council.

Evelyn and Paul Grant, both deceased, are survived by their three children and four grandchildren. Above, Evelyn is pictured in 1991 with her grandson Evan Michael Grant of Lake George, New York. (Courtesy of Paula Steger.)

On the cover: The daughters of Frederick and Julia Niesen pose with friends in the summer of 1895. Pictured here, from left to right, are Adela Niesen, Laura Niesen, unidentified, Clarice Bruere, and Paula Niesen. (Courtesy of Christine O'Shaughnessy.)

IMAGES
of America

RICHMOND HEIGHTS
1868–1940

Joellen Gamp McDonald and
Ruth Nichols Keenoy

ARCADIA
PUBLISHING

Copyright © 2006 by Joellen Gamp McDonald and Ruth Nichols Keenoy
ISBN 978-1-5316-2387-6

Published by Arcadia Publishing
Charleston, South Carolina

Library of Congress Catalog Card Number: 2006925383

For all general information contact Arcadia Publishing at:
Telephone 843-853-2070
Fax 843-853-0044
E-mail sales@arcadiapublishing.com
For customer service and orders:
Toll-Free 1-888-313-2665

Visit us on the Internet at www.arcadiapublishing.com

Richmond Heights Historical Society Members

Helen Abram	Leo and Pat Gamp	Helen Murray
Garvenia Attyberry	Virginia Louise Glover	Dele and Marylynn Oredugba
Jane and Robert Barker	Peter and Joane Griffin	Suzy Pfeifer and Kevin Mills
Kay and Larry Basta	Ken and Ronnie Heinz	Alice Provaznik
Bill Boyce	Stanley Henson	Rich and Joan Provaznik
Penney Bush Boyce	Michael and Barbara Jones	Rose Marie Renz
Ken and Ann Brune	Moses and Dorothy Jones	Roberta Rochester
Amy Brunsen	Phillip Jones	Andrew Rochman
Alice Bub	Patrick and Ruth Nichols Keenoy	St. Luke the Evangelist Parish
Sharon Calandro	Dr. Robert Koetting	Jim and Pat Scheidt
Leslie Canavan	Little Flower Parish	Sally Ann Sharamitaro
Lorraine Cates	Chris and Mary Martin	Julie Schulte
Herbert and Priscilla Cole	Kim and Jerry McCabe	Mark Telle – Telle Tire
Colombo Family	Tony and Joellen McDonald	Kenneth and Ruth Ann Thompkins
Florence Davis	Janice Mikesell	Rick and Cindy Vilcek
Paul DeFabio	Gannt and Kori Miller	Patricia Vilmer
Margaret Donnelly and David Riedel	Joseph Mullaney	Henrietta Williams
Andy and Lori Franke		Tom and Connie Williams

Listed here are the current members of the Richmond Heights Historical Society.

CONTENTS

ACKNOWLEDGMENTS

The Richmond Heights Historical Society Board of Directors—Alice Provaznik, Joellen McDonald, Joan Provaznik, Michael Jones, Barbara Jones, Moses Jones, Kim McCabe, Suzy Pfeifer, Rick Vilcek, Connie Williams, and Henrietta Williams—extend appreciation to the following people for assistance over the years: Evelyn Grant, founder and first president of the Richmond Heights Historical Society; the Richmond Heights City Council for financial support; Esley Hamilton, historian for St. Louis County Parks and Recreation; Sue Rehkopf for the initial organizing, indexing, and preserving of our collection and for training our volunteers; the Missouri Secretary of State's Office for a $5,000 grant; Jeanette Piquet, director of the Richmond Heights Memorial Library, for ongoing support; and regular volunteers Loraine Cates and Ruth Nichols Keenoy.

Donors to the archives include the following: Helen Abram, Roscoe Abram, Dr. Robert Altemeyer, Jerome Bollato, Ken Brune, Sharon Calandro, Lorraine Cates, Nelson Clark, Phyllis Cooper, Georgia Crenshaw, Jackie Dace, Marie DeBolt, Margaret Donnelly, Rick Ege, Frederick Fiddmont, Jerry and Agnes Flynn, Rena Foreman, Mary Frank, Andy Franke, Sidney Freund, Prof. Michael Fuller, Marion Gannon, George Gaskin, Jacob Gerber, Rich Gerding, Bruce Gerrie, Virginia Glover, James and Dudley Grove, Amy Hamilton, Ken Heinz, Arthur Hinch, the Historical Society of St. Louis County, Doug Houser, Anne Molasky Ibur, Irene Johnson, Lorraine Johnson, Barbara Jones, Henrietta Trieseler Jones, Michael Jones, Moses Jones, Jeanette Kaentor, Ruth Nichols Keenoy, Elyse McBride, Jerry and Kim McCabe, Joellen Gamp McDonald, Tony McDonald, Carmen Pace McFerren, Robert McKelvey, Cynthia Medart, Judy Metz, Mike Duffy's Bar and Grill, Korinne Miller, Helen Murray, fire chief Robert Niemeier, Christine O'Shaughnessy, Robert Pace, Paul and Jill Pagano, Thelma Pedrotti, Suzy Pfeifer, Sister Christian Price, Alice Provaznik, Joan Provaznik, Dave Reary, Sue Rehkopf, Tony and Angie Ribaudo, Andrew Rochman, Louis Roeder, Albert Rose, Georgia Rusan, Alberta Rutherford, Maggie Ryan, Jim Scheidt, Julie Schulte, Jennifer Scott, Mary Kay Scott, Tracey Scott, Second Baptist Church, Mary Seematter, Eugene and Gladys Slaughter, Jo Ann Smith, Sarah Splaun, Pat Sullivan, Edna Miller Taylor, Mark Telle, Rick Vilcek, Pat Vilmer, Lillie Mae Warner, Juanita Watson, Mary Watson, Bill and Janet Weber, Charles White, Mary Whorton, Virgil and Rosemary Wiesner, Lawrence Wilfong, Thelma Willis, and Cecelia Wollbrinck.

For their direct involvement in preparing this book for publication, we thank the following: Barbara Jones, Michael Jones, Moses Jones, Ruth Nichols Keenoy, Joellen Gamp McDonald, Alice Provaznik, Joan Provaznik, Georgia Rusan, and Rick Vilcek for contacting resources; Lorraine Cates, Ruth Nichols Keenoy, and Joellen Gamp McDonald for research; Tom Williams and Bobby Jones for scanning; Bill Boyce, Ruth Nichols Keenoy, and Kim McCabe for photography; and Ruth Nichols Keenoy and Joellen Gamp McDonald for writing.

Publishing a list creates the unfortunate possibility that a name or donation may be missed. For any such omissions we extend our sincerest apologies.

INTRODUCTION

The people who live in Richmond Heights are its most interesting and important asset. Early residents brought individual and lasting impressions that make the community unlike any other. It may be said that Richmond Heights was an early suburb of the city of St. Louis. In some respects this is true. The community was established outside of St. Louis's city limits and, by the early 20th century, had gained prominence as a municipality. Richmond Heights began to take shape as a residential sector even earlier, however, at about the same time that St. Louis was anticipating its centennial celebration, the Louisiana Exposition (more commonly known as the 1904 World's Fair). Today, there remain many physical reminders of Richmond Heights's early years. With each passing year, many such edifices "disappear" as the city continues to burgeon and prosper. This publication provides a limited glimpse into the early history of Richmond Heights and celebrates the people who have made it unique.

Richmond Heights is located in St. Louis County, bordered to the east by the independent city of St. Louis, to the north by Clayton, to the south by Maplewood, and to the west by Brentwood and Ladue. As noted above, the community started its development during the late 19th century. One early developer was Frederick E. Niesen, a local grocer who later worked as a real estate agent. In 1892, Niesen constructed a large home for his family near the present location of St. Luke the Evangelist Church at Dale and Bellevue Avenues. Much of this area was part of a large parcel known as the Gratiot League Square. Gratiot Square, gained by Charles Gratiot in 1798, encompassed "nearly three miles square (5,712 acres), the largest grant ever made by the Spanish near the village" of St. Louis. Following Gratiot's death in 1817, the parcel was divided among his heirs.

During the 1850s, the former Gratiot League Square was again subdivided when the (Missouri) Pacific Railroad Company began construction on a railroad linking St. Louis and Kansas City. Although connections with Kansas City remained incomplete until after the Civil War, the line extended west from downtown St. Louis to the Cheltenham area (east of Richmond Heights) by 1852. Local streetcar lines were extended into the vicinity of Richmond Heights as electric trolleys by the 1890s, which helped to open the area to early residential development. These early streetcars provided access to amusement parks such as West End Heights and Forest Park Highlands. Essential during the world's fair, they remained in use for many years. Several subdivisions were created shortly after the arrival of the streetcar, including Bellevue Square, which supported an early center of commerce situated north of Dale Avenue along the west side of Bellevue Avenue.

Before 1912, the area that would become Richmond Heights held 18 families, including the Niesen, Brennan, Bruno, Buehning, DeBolt, Gay, Grove, and McCutchan families. The impact of the upcoming 1904 St. Louis World's Fair was significant to the community's growth and early development. The event sparked interest in real estate, and St. Louis further extended its streetcar lines to provide direct service to the fair site. Many homes in and around Richmond

Heights were constructed using salvaged materials from the demolition of properties built for this event. At least two homes within the city's limits today were constructed to house fair employees during the exposition. Although the city would see its most tremendous growth rate during the 1920s and 1930s, the events surrounding the world's fair brought much attention and interest to the young community.

There is much debate about how the area came to be known as Richmond Heights. The local legend that the name is associated with Civil War general Robert E. Lee, who served as a surveyor for the Army Corps of Engineers in St. Louis, appears to be mere speculation. Some believe that early residents, reminded of the southern landscape, named the community for Virginia's capital city. Regardless, from its inception, Richmond Heights was developed exclusively as a residential neighborhood, often called "the City of Friendly Homes." Statistics from 1946 indicate that of the community's 1,381 acres, more than 50 percent were developed for single-family residences. Only three percent of the city was commercially zoned, primarily limited to major streets such as Bellevue Avenue, Big Bend Boulevard, and Clayton Road. Even less prominent was industry, which comprised a very minor percentage of the city's total land use.

Richmond Heights was incorporated in 1913, at which time the city encompassed the area bounded by the St. Louis city limits to the east, Wise Avenue to the north, Big Bend Boulevard to the west, and near present-day Hiawatha and Glades Avenues to the south. Additional annexations occurred when the city expanded west to Hanley Road and north to Clayton Road in 1918, north to Oakland Avenue in 1920, south to Bruno Avenue between Big Bend Boulevard and the St Louis's city limits in 1922, west to Brentwood Boulevard in 1925, and finally west to Lay Road in 1928. Population statistics continued to rise steadily throughout the early-to-mid-20th century, with recorded estimates of 2,135 residents in 1920; 9,150 in 1930; 12,802 in 1940; and 15,045 in 1950. The city's largest number of residents was recorded in 1960 as 15,622, a number that has been steadily diminishing due to commercial development and interstate highway construction.

As noted, this publication is intended to encourage preservation of the city's abundant history, much of which remains a puzzle. As such, the authors request that individuals who may have missing pieces contact the Richmond Heights Historical Society to share their memories, stories, and any cherished photographs that they are willing to allow us to copy for our collection. If you wish to join in our endeavor, please write or call us in care of the city of Richmond Heights, 1330 South Big Bend Boulevard, Richmond Heights, Missouri 63117; (314) 645-0404. Please send e-mail via the city's website, http://www.richmondheights.org. A membership form is available on that site.

One

EARLY RESIDENTS

During the 1800s, landowners such as William McCutchan, Henry and Elizabeth Barron, Edward and Livinia Gay, Frederick and Julia Niesen, John W. Ranken, Charles and Mary Rannells, and John and Victorine Bruno built homes on large estates. As St. Louis prepared for the 1904 world's fair, some of these landholdings were subdivided. A July 13, 1901, account in the *St. Louis Daily Globe-Democrat* credits the John W. Ranken Realty Company with giving Richmond Heights its name in mid-1890. The article continues, "It is likely that a corporation will be formed to handle the property in time for the world's fair activity this fall [comprised of Frederick Niesen and] other well-known business men [who] have their home places at and near Richmond Heights."

Dwellings at 7333, 7347, and 7403 (now 7405) Wise Avenue were built to house fair workers and/or attendees. After the fair, Frederick Niesen began developing Sunset Hill on part of his estate. Entrepreneurs such as James Brennan built homes for their families. After Rannells Farm was subdivided, some of the property was purchased by Evens and Howard Brickworks. There, the company would build worker homes to entice African American families to the area as a labor pool. While the McCutchans retained some of their landholdings, the Barron property changed hands a number of times until Levi and Lucy Childress bought it in 1915.

Amenities including electricity, sewers, and piped water were gradually introduced in the early 1900s. Residents prevailed upon the first board of aldermen to loosen restrictions on commercial developments, allowing businesses such as Schulte's Market and Riley's Hardware to open.

By the 1920s, Richmond Heights's proximity to St. Louis City, its improvements in infrastructure, access to public transportation, and a booming economy made the community a haven for families seeking life outside the inner city.

Commerce continued to develop. The city gained its own hospital when St. Mary's, designed by architect Albert B. Groves, opened in 1924. While the Great Depression played a hand in slowing expansion, Richmond Heights benefitted from Civil Works Administration projects that channeled creeks and springs and provided more sewer systems. By 1932, population growth enabled Richmond Heights to petition for status as a third-class city. Just before World War II, housing construction boomed again. The Manhassett Village apartment complex was designed by Perston J. Bradshaw and completed by H. B. Deal and Company in 1939, and in 1940 the Kubatskys developed housing for middle-class families in Hanley Downs.

Mary Buchroeder poses with her daughters Peg (left) and Ellie. The Buchroeder family moved to 7515 Harter Avenue in 1919. (Courtesy of Marion Buchroeder Gannon.)

The Barron-Childress House was razed in 2003 by the Second Baptist Church, owner of the property. Italianate in design, it was built in 1868 by Henry and Elizabeth Barron. During the 1920s, when the home was owned by Levi and Lucy Childress, columns and other Greek Revival features were added to the structure. (Courtesy of the Richmond Heights Historical Society Collection.)

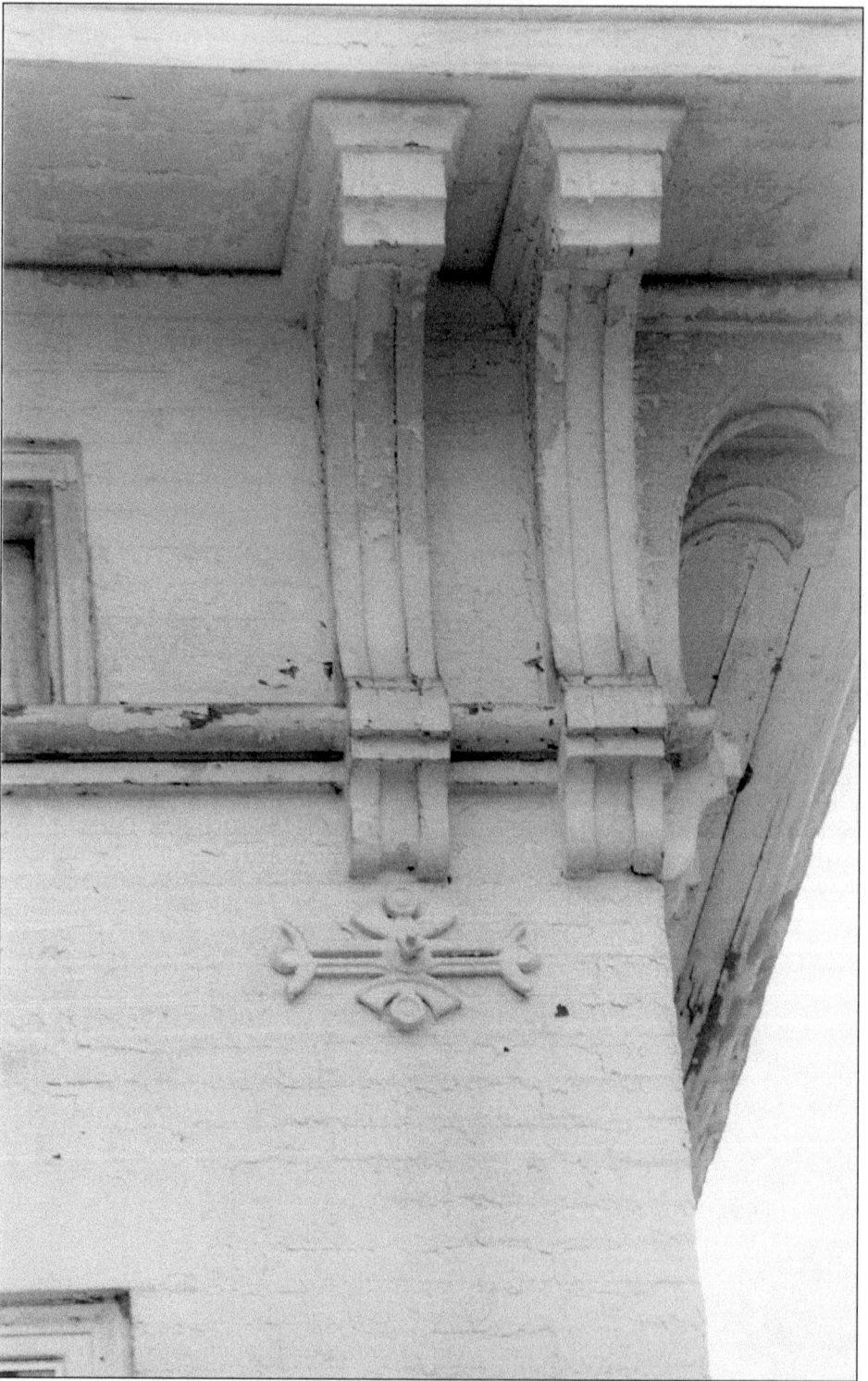

These architectural details form the roof line of the Barron-Childress House. (Courtesy of Doug Houser.)

The builder of the Barron House, Dr. Henry Barron, was a St. Louis dentist and founder of the St. Louis Dental Society. (Courtesy of Prof. Michael Fuller.)

According to St. Louis County Parks and Recreation hustorian Esley Hamilton, in 1866, William T. McCutchan sold 32 acres of his property to his sister Elizabeth McCutchan Barron (seen here) and her husband, Dr. Henry Barron. They are believed to have built the Italianate house in 1868. In 1876, foreclosure on a loan forced the couple to move to Webster Groves. The house underwent significant architectural changes in the 1920s, when owned by Levi Wade and Lucy Turner Childress. In 1954, the Second Baptist Church purchased the land and eventually demolished the house in 2003. (Courtesy of Prof. Michael Fuller.)

A decorative iron anchor was removed from the Barron-Childress House. All of the structure's iron anchors were manufactured in St. Louis by the Pullis Brothers. (Courtesy of Doug Houser.)

RICHMOND HEIGHTS

EST. 1982

HISTORICAL SOCIETY

Where the past comes to life

Jerry McCabe modeled the logo for the Richmond Heights Historical Society after the iron anchor removed from the Barron-Childress House. The original anchor is part of the archives as a gift from Bruce Gerrie to Doug Houser.

The Gay Villa appears here in a copy of an undated photograph. The land which currently houses both Hampton Park and Lake Forest can be connected to the Gay family even before 1862, when the tract was purchased by John H. Gay. John's son Edward likely built the three-story Italianate villa sometime between 1857 and 1862. Edward was married to Lavinia Gay, and while they spent most of the year at St. Louis Plantation at Plaquemine, Iberville, Louisiana, their summers were spent in St. Louis. Edward died in 1889, and Lavinia in 1891. (Courtesy of the Richmond Heights Historical Society Collection.)

The home of John Baptist Bruno and Victorine Verrier Bruno stands at 7310 Bruno Avenue. The couple built their house in unincorporated territory in St. Louis County in 1890. John Bruno came to St. Louis from France with his parents as a young child. Upon John's death in 1917, there were 13 surviving Bruno children: Lou, married to Faith Deno; Polyte "Pete"; John B. "Jack"; August "Gus," married to Ida Lightfoot; Charley, married to Frances Dorste; Alfred "Fritz"; Jim; Marie "Mary," married to Leon Boulicault; Adeline, married to Frank Leek; Julia, married to Charles Richert; Victorine, married to John Vogel; Josephine "Josie," married to John Gannett; and Eugenia "Jennie." The Bruno Farm was subdivided following the death of Mrs. Bruno. The land was annexed by Richmond Heights in 1922, at a hastily called night meeting of the board of aldermen before the city of Maplewood could do so. (Courtesy of the Richmond Heights Historical Society Collection.)

The Greek Revival home of Charles S. and Mary Warder Rannells is pictured here in 1907. The Rannells Farm, called Woodside, is the last remnant of the agrarian lifestyle of the Anglo-Americans who settled in the area before the Civil War. The Rannells brought with them a large contingent of family and some slaves when they moved to Woodside in 1850. Ironically, much of the Rannells' land in Richmond Heights later became part of the city's historic African American neighborhood. This narrative taken from the historic nomination of the Rannells home in 2005, prepared by Kris Zapalac, Ph.D. (Courtesy of Doug Houser and Greg Rannells.)

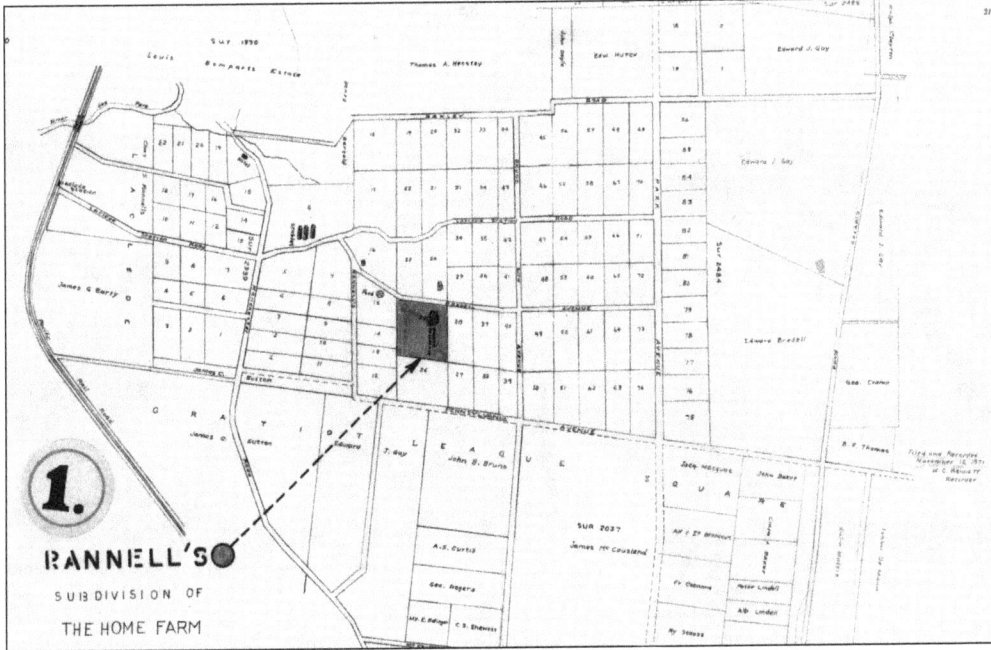

In this 1871 plat map of the Rannells Farm, family land holdings span from Maplewood into Richmond Heights. Some of the lots shown were purchased by the Evens and Howard Brickworks in the early 1900s. The company then began building small worker houses for African American families here in 1907. (Courtesy of the Richmond Heights Historical Society Collection.)

Two of the Niesen daughters pose in the front yard of the family home in this undated photograph. There were three Niesen daughters: Adela (born 1881), Laura (born 1883), and Paula (born 1884). (Courtesy of Christine O'Shaughnessy.)

FRONTIER COURT

BELLEVUE AVENUE

The Niesen family compound, seen here, was called Frontier Court. There is no evidence that four additional homes were actually built on this five-acre plot. However, Frederick Niesen did built two houses for his daughters when they were married, Laura to Harold Kramer and Paula to Joseph Forshaw. Frederick Niesen and his sons-in-law were active in civic affairs in the community. (Courtesy of the Richmond Heights Historical Society Collection.)

Frederick Niesen was 75 years old when this photograph was taken. (Courtesy of Christine O'Shaughnessy.)

In 1880, Frederick Niesen married Julia Ambs Niesen. Julia, pictured in 1880, was a descendant of the Uhrig Brewing family. The couple built a wooden mansion on the highest point of their 40 acres in Richmond Heights, moving there in 1892. There were 18 families living in the area at that time. Julia died in 1948, and Frederick in 1952. In the mid-1950s, the State of Missouri took the estate in order to build the Daniel Boone Expressway, now Interstate 64/40. (Courtesy of Christine O'Shaughnessy.)

Walter Buehning moved his wife and two daughters into their new home, located at 1701 Bellevue Avenue, on October 19, 1899. (Courtesy of the Richmond Heights Historical Society Collection.)

Florence (left) and Irene Buehning stand on the front porch of the family home, the Walter H. Buehning House. Buehning was the first president of the Richmond Heights Governing League and a charter member of the Richmond Heights Presbyterian Church. In 1927, following the murder of chief marshal George McCready while on duty, Walter served as acting marshal until a permanent replacement could be hired. This narrative and photograph were taken from the 1963 Richmond Heights 50th anniversary booklet.

Miss Florence Buehning (l.) and Miss Irene Buehning on front steps of their home.

James and Bridget Brennan constructed their family home at 7303 Hoover Avenue in 1909. (Courtesy of the Richmond Heights Historical Society Collection.)

Photographed at their 1902 wedding are James Brennan and Bridget Noonan. (Courtesy of Mary Kay Scott.)

James Brennan sports formal attire while holding his prize rooster. According to Mae Brennan Gannon and Dorothy Brennan Hartman, "When James and Bridget Brennan moved to 7303 Hoover Avenue in 1909, daughter Mary Mae was already born. Eventually there would be three more Brennan children: Austin, James, and Dorothy. Unlike others on the block, they had indoor plumbing and two telephones—a Kinloch and a Bell." (Courtesy of Mary Kay Scott.)

Mae Brennan appears in her eighth-grade graduation photograph in 1920. (Courtesy of Mary Kay Scott.)

Mae Brennan Gannon poses with her two sons, Frank and baby James, in 1920. Mae married Frank E. Gannon, and they raised their family in Richmond Heights. Frank E. Gannon served as the city attorney from 1930 to 1935. (Courtesy of Mary Kay Scott.)

Marguerite Grove stands on the veranda of the Hampton Park family estate, located at 1108 Hillside Drive, in 1921. Pictured with their mother are James Henry (standing), Edwin Wiley "Bill," and Gertrude Matthewson Grove. (Courtesy of Cynthia Medart.)

The Grove estate covered 40 acres, which included the house, greenhouse, and extensive gardens designed by Peter Selsor. Dr. Edwin Wiley Grove Sr. moved his family to St. Louis from Tennessee in the 1890s. A pharmacist, he developed a number of very successful patented medicines such as Grove's Tasteless Chill Tonic and Bromoquinine. His son Edwin Wiley Grove Jr. married Marguerite Cefalu of New Orleans. They built their home in 1916. (Courtesy of Cynthia Medart.)

Marion and Ken Gannon stand in the center, behind a dancing couple, at their wedding in 1940. Everyone is gathered outside Le Chateau, where the group would have the wedding dinner. (Courtesy of Marion Buchroeder Gannon.)

In 1940, Marion Gannon stands beside the car and in front of the family's rental apartment at 1322A Hawthorne Avenue. Marion Buchroeder married Kenrick Gannon in 1940, and they moved into their first apartment on Bellevue and West Park (Dale Avenue) in Richmond Heights. In 1943, they bought a home at 7162 Wise Avenue. The Gannons raised six children: David, Steven, Patricia, John "Tim," Theresa, and Barbara. (Courtesy of Marion Buchroeder Gannon.)

Sisters Flo (left) and Peggy Buchroeder play "battling solitaire" in the backyard of the family home, located at 7447 Harter Avenue (originally 7515 Harter Avenue), in 1940. Charles Buchroeder Jr. and Mary Evelyn Buchroeder moved to 7515 Harter Avenue in Richmond Heights in 1919. They raised a family of seven girls and three boys, sending all of them through the Maplewood-Richmond Heights school system. In birth order, their children are as follows: Evelyn, Mildred, Richard, Florence, Bill, Bob, Marion "Mae," Eleanor "Ellie," Peggy, and Mary. (Courtesy of Marion Buchroeder Gannon.)

Joseph Pedrotti and Thelma Morrison were married at Immaculate Conception Church in Maplewood in 1938. (Courtesy of Julie Pedrotti Schulte and Maggie Pedrotti Ryan.)

Joe and Thelma Pedrotti pose in front of their home at 7445 Ethel Avenue with daughters Maggie (left) and Julie. Thelma Morrison grew up in Maplewood. After the couple married, they bought their first and only home at 7445, where they raised their four children. Thelma was a great contributor to the historical society. She was co-chairwoman for the Meals on Wheels card party for over 20 years, a member of the Hadley Township Democratic Club, and on the committee for the 75th anniversary of Richmond Heights. (Courtesy of Julie Pedrotti Schulte and Maggie Pedrotti Ryan.)

Charles A. Lindbergh (left) and Harlan "Bud" Gurney stand in front of a Standard F-1 plane on April 9, 1922, during their barnstorming days. That same month, they took their first airplane ride together when Lindbergh enrolled as a student at the Nebraska Aircraft School in Lincoln. Later, Lindbergh and Gurney performed parachute drops and stunt flying together at fairs. They made their first visit to St. Louis in 1923 to attend the International Air Races and then worked together at Lambert Field. (Courtesy of the Charles A. Lindbergh Photograph Collection, Missouri Historical Society.)

For a short time in 1923, Lindbergh rented a room from the Rescia family at 1414 Big Bend Boulevard in Richmond Heights. After his historic flight across the Atlantic Ocean in 1927, the city changed the name of Maryland Avenue to Lindbergh Drive in his honor. (Courtesy of the Richmond Heights Historical Society Collection.)

Two

CITY GOVERNMENT

Incorporated on December 29, 1913, Richmond Heights became a fourth-class city with a mayor and eight aldermen. James M. O'Keefe was appointed mayor in 1912. Following incorporation, James M. Jensen was elected mayor and served seven terms of office. An early distinction for the city occurred in 1926, when Mary Hoffman was elected to the board of aldermen, becoming the first woman voted into such a position in St. Louis County.

In 1912, city marshal Louis Gloeckner was sworn in along with other officials. He resigned in 1914 and was replaced by a marshal Dilk, with the mayor, city clerk and aldermen being sworn in as Dilk's deputies. Before the year was out, T. S. Casey was appointed to replace Dilk. From 1915 to 1919, W. Ziegenmeyer served as marshal, replaced by George W. McCready. He was killed while he walked his beat on Bellevue Avenue. Walter Buehning filled in as marshal until John Maloney was elected to this position in 1923. Maloney was in charge of street work and the police department, earning $150 a year for both jobs. The police department was organized into a 24-hour-a-day, 365-day-a-year agency during the 1920s. In 1924, police telephone boxes were installed throughout the city, and two night officers were hired. The department moved into city hall in 1927. Thomas Florence became the next chief in 1928. In the early 1930s, three clerks were hired to provide 24-hour coverage. When Thomas H. Brown became chief in 1932, the city abolished the fee system for police and marshals.

Ted Hart became the city's sole official volunteer firefighter. He drove the truck and recruited help at the scene. Charles Knickerbocker remembered the following: "Ninety-five percent of all fires were weed fires in the fall of the year. The city did not have fire plugs at this time. These weed fires were put out by beating them with a section of old hose nailed over a piece of two-by-four." In 1926, the city established a paid fire department with David Parshall as chief and three other firemen. The next year, the department moved from Ted Hart's garage at Big Bend Boulevard and Ethel Avenue to the new city hall at Big Bend Boulevard and Dale Avenue. In 1927, the city added a new chief, Panser, and an Ahern Fox pumper. In 1930, John Frossard began a 10-year stint as fire chief. He was followed by George Hawkins, who served from 1940 to 1954. In 1928, when Ira B. Sargent became chief, the department adopted a mascot named Freckles. When he missed a run on the fire truck, the fox terrier would pout and refuse any petting. He was stuffed in 1937, remaining for many years in the Richmond Heights Library until he mysteriously disappeared in the early 1960s.

When the Richmond Heights Lions Club disbanded in 1933 due to the Great Depression, it donated its remaining $16 to the city for the start of a library. Citizens added to this small beginning with 1,800 books gathered from door-to-door collections, and the library began in a tiny upstairs room in city hall at Big Bend Boulevard and Dale Avenue. Citizens approved a 3¢ per $100 assessed value tax to support the library. A Mr. Wentworth served as the first president of the board of trustees, and in 1935, Marguerite Norville was hired as the first librarian.

In 1932, with a population of 10,000, Richmond Heights petitioned the state for third-class status and changed to a commission form of government. At this time, a mayor and three commissioners served in leadership roles, but a few years later a fourth commissioner was added when the population exceeded 12,000 residents.

In 1931, city hall was literally half its present size. Housing all departments, it quickly became too small, and in 1935 an addition doubled the building's capacity. (Courtesy of the Richmond Heights Historical Society Collection.)

In 1931, the Citizen's Smoke Abatement League sent this letter to city officials regarding the air pollution caused by the furnace at city hall. (Courtesy of the Richmond Heights Historical Society Collection.

Richmond Heights—Niesen Tract in 1888—Looking southwest from Bellevue and Dale

City of Richmond Heights

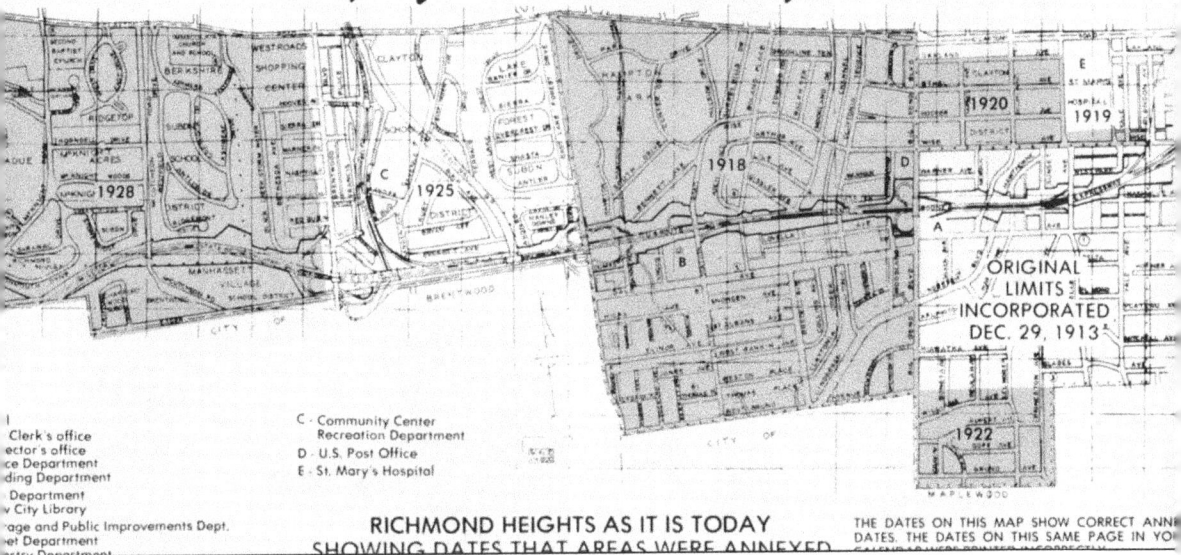

Clerk's office
ector's office
ce Department
ding Department
Department
v City Library
age and Public Improvements Dept.
et Department
stry Department

C - Community Center
    Recreation Department
D - U.S. Post Office
E - St. Mary's Hospital

RICHMOND HEIGHTS AS IT IS TODAY
SHOWING DATES THAT AREAS WERE ANNEXED

THE DATES ON THIS MAP SHOW CORRECT ANN
DATES. THE DATES ON THIS SAME PAGE IN YO

The development of new residential sectors escalated as the Niesen Tract (pictured above), Bruno Farm, Gay Villa, and the Childress estate were subdivided. While the Grove family retained their estate and extensive gardens, other homes were constructed in the Hampton Park vicinity. As pictured above, the city limits expanded through a series of annexations until the northern boundary of Richmond Heights became Clayton Road; the western boundary reached the east side of Lay Road; and the southern boundary included the Bruno Farm up to Big Bend, then followed West Bruno Avenue to Hanley Road. Continuing, the southern line ran up the north side of Eager Road to its end and angle northwest to the east side of Lay Road. The last annexation occurred in 1928. (Courtesy of the Richmond Heights Historical Society Collection.)

The first mayor of Richmond Heights, James O'Keefe, served from 1912 to 1913, when James Jenson was elected as a replacement. (Courtesy of the Richmond Heights Historical Society Collection.)

Richmond Heights voters elected James Jenson to seven terms in office, spanning the years 1913 to 1926. (Courtesy of the Richmond Heights Historical Society Collection.)

Resident Oliver Hast launched a political campaign against Mayor Jensen in 1926. In a hotly contested election, Jensen was defeated by Edward J. Houlihan, who won by just two votes. (Courtesy of the Richmond Heights Historical Society Collection.)

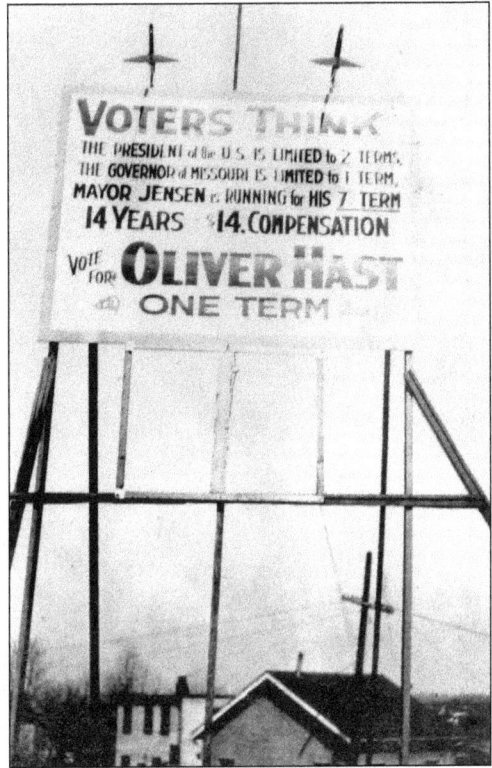

Mayor Edward J. Houlihan served from 1926 to 1930. (Courtesy of the Richmond Heights Historical Society Collection.)

Henry Krallman held the position of mayor from 1930 to 1932. In 1932, a commission form of government was installed following the city's change in status from a fourth- to a third-class city. (Courtesy of the Richmond Heights Historical Society Collection.)

John J. Flanagan served as mayor for one year, in 1932. (Courtesy of the Richmond Heights Historical Society Collection.)

Mayor Brainerd LaTourette Sr., elected in 1932, was retained in office by voters for 16 years. (Courtesy of the Richmond Heights Historical Society Collection.)

Henry Trieseler was the city attorney during the 1920s and early 1930s. He also served as a state representative from Richmond Heights. (Courtesy of Henrietta Trieseler Jones.)

RICHMOND HEIGHTS CITY AND BUSINESS DIRECTORY 1930

CITY OFFICIALS

Mayor – Edward J. Houlihan..1516 Del Norte Ave.
City Attorney – H. G. Trieseler...1415 Silverton Place
Prosecuting Attorney – Frank Gannon.......................................7336 Ethel Ave.
City Clerk – George H. Skillman...7367 La Veta Ave.
Collector – Celeste C. Tripp..7366 Arlington Drive
Marshal – Thomas J. Florence..7154 Wise Ave.
Police Judge – Jerome Simon..7213 West Park Ave.
Assistant Chief – Thomas Brown...7539 Dale Ave.
Chief of fire Department – Ira Sargent......................................7400 Hoover Ave.
Auditor – W. H. Cline...1410 Woodland Drive
Treasurer – J. A. McCue...1724 Beulah Place

COMMISSIONERS

Plumbing Commissioner – F. D. Albin.......................................7417 Hiawatha Ave.
Deputy Plumbing Commissioner – Eugene Gartland.....................1285 Arch Terrace
Electrical Inspector – H. H. Talbot..7310 Hoover Ave.
Building Commissioner – J. P. Stuckes......................................1104 Yale Ave.
Street Commissioner – John J. Leslie.......................................7725a Arthur Ave.

ALDERMEN

First Ward   Albert Reilly..7208 Dale Ave.
                Lawrence Riegel..7232 Delta Ave.

Second Ward   M. B. Stevens...1336 Highland Terrace
                John Angthius..7421 Dale Ave.

Third Ward   Bart J. Lyster...1713 Bonita Ave.
                Charles H. DuBois..1706 Big Bend Blvd.

Fourth Ward   James A. Brennan..7303 Hoover Ave.
                Glenn R. McCarty...1111 Blendon Place

Fifth Ward   John J. Flanagan...1247 Boland Place
                August Spahn...7717 Weston Place

TELEPHONE CALLS

Police Department............................HIland 3000
City Clerk – Collector........................HIland 3000
Fire (ONLY)....................................HIland 4000

Board of Aldermen Meet Regularly Second Wednesday Each Month,
City Hall, Big Bend. Blvd. and Dale Ave., 8 P.M.

Pictured here is a page from the Richmond Heights City and Business Directory of 1930.

Officials and police officers pose by the first automated emergency signal at Clayton Road and Big Bend Boulevard. Prior to the installation of this system, when an emergency vehicle was sent out, the dispatcher had to call the Mobil station and tell an attendant to run across the street and throw the switch to stop traffic. Seen here in the first row, from left to right, are Richmond Heights mayor Brainerd LaTourette Sr. (throwing the switch), Clayton mayor Charles Shaw, unidentified, and Richmond Heights police chief Thomas Brown. Others have been identified as Richmond Heights police officer Buck Rogers, officer Glen Forrestal, and motorcycle patrolman Grant Simmons. (Courtesy of the Richmond Heights Historical Society Collection.)

Marshal George W. McCready, pictured here in 1920, was killed in the line of duty on July 2, 1922. A street in the southern part of the city is named in his memory. (Courtesy of the Richmond Heights Historical Society Collection.)

Police officers posing in 1939 are as follows, from left to right: (first row) Oliver Brueggeman, Sgt. Grant Simmons, an unidentified lieutenant, Chief Thomas Brown, Sgt. Dick Sherman, and Rick Ryan; (second row) Frank Noges, James Riley, Dick Carter, William Hummel, Red Greggerson, and John Baldas. (Courtesy of the Richmond Heights Police Department.)

This undated photograph shows members of the police department. (Courtesy of the Richmond Heights Police Department.)

Richmond Heights's first fire truck, a Model T, was purchased in 1922 and housed in Ted Hart's garage on Ethel Avenue near Big Bend Boulevard. Jim Hugger (left) and Rodney Hart are seen in this photograph. Until 1922, all fire fighting had been carried out by those nearby the blazes. (Courtesy of the Richmond Heights Historical Society Collection.)

This undated photograph shows the first fire truck, a Model T. (Courtesy of the Richmond Heights Historical Society Collection.)

Members of the 1930–1931 fire department were as follows, from left to right: (first row) John Frossard, Freckles, and John Keelan; (second row) Larry Sargent, George Hawkins, Herbert Lehmer, and Andrew Markey. The fire truck in the background is a 1926 Aherns Fox pumper. (Courtesy of the Richmond Heights Historical Society Collection.)

At the desk of the Richmond Heights Library in 1939 is librarian Edna Amend. A mounted Freckles stands in the center. Nearby at the table, librarian Marguerite Norville reads to children. Standing in the stacks is board president Mr. Wentworth. (Courtesy of the Richmond Heights Historical Society Collection.)

This 1940 library display features scouting-related artifacts. (Courtesy of the Richmond Heights Historical Society Collection.)

Three

CHURCHES

Even before Richmond Heights became a city, early residents worked hard to form congregations and bring religious worship into the community. Although the Richmond Heights Presbyterian Church was the first to incorporate, in 1907, it was quickly followed by Mount Zion Missionary Baptist Church, the Church of the Living God, and St. Luke the Evangelist Church, all before the city had celebrated its first anniversary. Short narratives are included with each photograph of a church formed before 1940. It is important to note that outside of the years chronicled in this book, four other congregations opened their doors in the Richmond Heights community: Luther Memorial Church in 1942, the Church of the Immacolata in 1945, the Second Baptist Church in 1954, and Brith Sholom Kneseth Israel Synagogue in 1960.

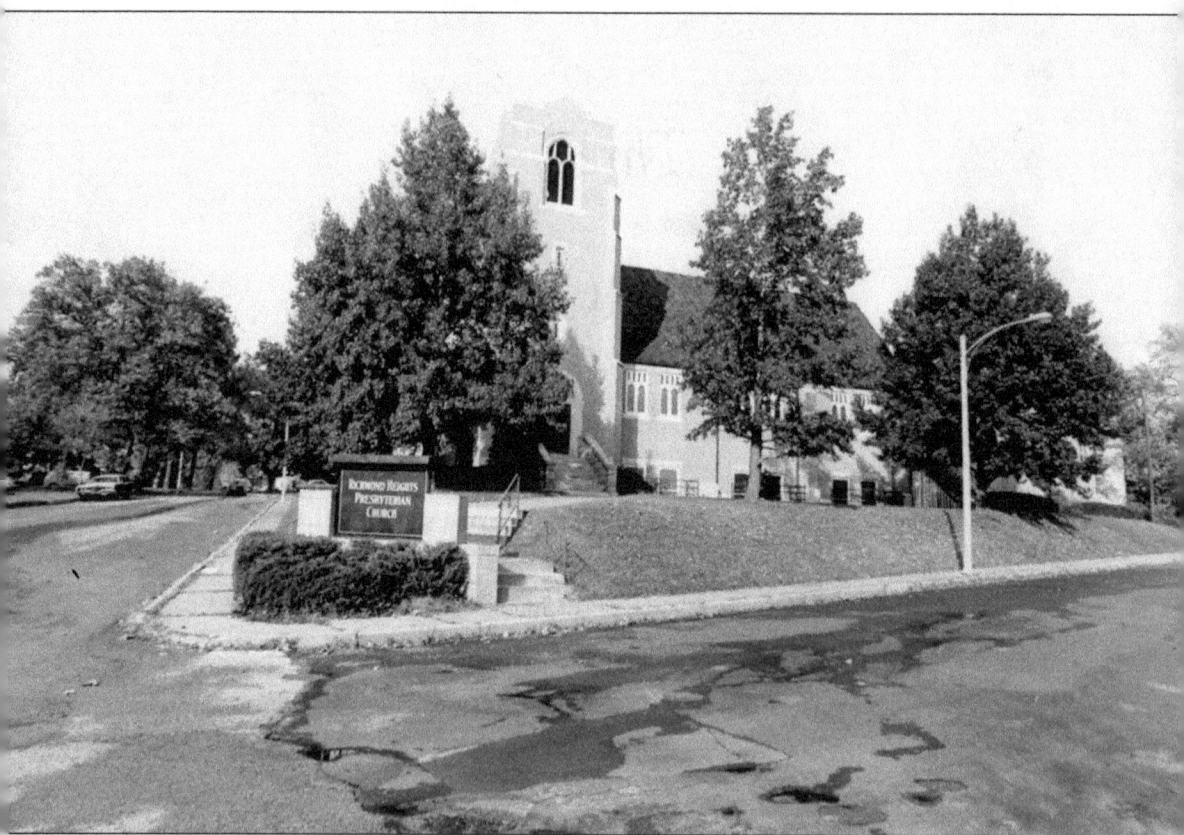

In 1907, three couples started a Sunday school in the Richmond Heights School. When an objection was made to the building being used for religious purposes, a residence at 7228 Arlington was made available, rent free. Two kerosene lamps, a small stove, and a load of coal were purchased. Benches were built by members. Later, an organ was added. At this time, there were 50 to 60 church members, and ministers of various denominations preached at Richmond Heights Presbyterian. In 1910, a church site on Pennsylvania (Big Bend Boulevard) was obtained. In 1915, the superstructure of that building was completed. Rev. O. L. Pride was pastor. A permanent pastor, Rev. H. B. Phillips, was installed on November 26, 1922. The present site, at Silverton Place and Lindbergh Drive (7339 Lindbergh Drive), was purchased in 1924 and the sanctuary was dedicated in 1926, but the church building was not fully completed until 1949. Mildrid H. Rice recorded this history in 1929. (Courtesy of the Richmond Heights Historical Society Collection.)

Mount Zion Missionary Baptist Church, located at 1500 South Hanley Road, was incorporated in 1911. At that time, the area was called South Clayton. The present site is the third Richmond Heights location for the congregation. At first, members worshiped in St. Mark's Methodist Church, at 8022 Dale Avenue. From 1926 to 1958, members attended services in the basement of a building at 1628 South Hanley Road. Finally, in October 1958, the current building was opened. Rev. James E. Fiddmont, pictured with his wife and family in chapter 7, served as pastor for 32 years. The property where the church now stands was once operated as a park by the United Negro Liberation League. The Marcus Garvey Group of Mohammedans maintained the grounds and charged a fee for its use. Groups such as the Pink Tea Ladies rented the park to hold political meetings and host cotillions. Because of Redevelopment in this area, the church structure is set to be razed in 2007. (Courtesy of the Richmond Heights Historical Society Collection.)

The Church of the Living God, Temple No. 29, was formerly located at 8021 Dale Avenue. (Courtesy of the Richmond Heights Historical Society Collection.)

CHURCH OF THE LIVING GOD

CHRISTIAN WORKERS FOR FELLOWSHIP

F. C. SCOTT
Chief Bishop

W. E. CRUMES
Presiding Bishop

J. A. MOSELY
Pastor

8021 DALE AVE   **RICHMOND HEIGHTS, MO**

In 1912–1913, the Church of the Living God congregation began meeting in a tent on Eager Road. At that time, the pastor was Elder James M. Taylor. Pioneer members included Bessie Hollins, Jennie Eddings, Ella Lawrence, Lee Lawrence, J. L. Malone, Berry Burke, Georgia Burke, Zelma Ferris, James Eddings, Frank Rusan, Sally Rusan, and Sister Cannon. The congregation moved to the Eddings home in 1913 and, in 1916, purchased the property at 8021 Dale Avenue for its church. The building burned to the ground in 1946 and was rebuilt at that same location. In the late 1990s, in order to construct the Richmond Heights Community Center on the former church property, the city provided the congregation with a structure at 8016 Dale Avenue. This church is also set to be razed due to redevelopment in 2007. (Courtesy of the Richmond Heights Historical Society Collection.)

Shown here is St. Luke the Evangelist Catholic Church. In 1914, Rev. Joseph Collins became the first priest assigned to determine if a parish could be established in Richmond Heights. The first Mass was celebrated at the old Benoist homestead on October 11, 1914, with 175 people present. A house at 29 Sunset Avenue was purchased that same year and served as a chapel until 1915, when property at Bellevue and Delta Avenues (7237 Delta Avenue) was purchased as a site. In 1916, a groundbreaking ceremony celebrated the building of a combination church and school. The present church, Norman Gothic in style, was constructed in 1929 at the southeast corner of Bellevue and Dale Avenues, during the tenure of Rev. Joseph McMahon. In 1940, the Caen stone altar was installed. (Courtesy of the Richmond Heights Historical Society Collection.)

The Church of the Little Flower was built on land purchased by Archbishop John Glennon in 1925. The original parishioners approved the name Little Flower in honor of St. Therese of Lisieux, who had been canonized that same year. Fr. Joseph Tammany was assigned as the first pastor. There were few homes in the area, and thus only 40 families in the new parish. Nevertheless, a structure deemed "the Cardboard Cathedral" was hastily constructed and the first mass was said at midnight on December 24, 1925. A rectory was added in 1931. The present church, dedicated in 1949 and located at Boland Place and Arch Terrace, was modeled after another church built in the round in Royal Oak, Michigan. (Courtesy of the Richmond Heights Historical Society Collection.)

The First Church of God congregation began as a prayer group in 1927, meeting in the home of Brother and Sister Tucker at 1632 Stockard. The group attended church at the Garfield Congregation in St. Louis City. After a number of temporary locations, the members purchased property at 8011 Elinore Avenue and asked Sr. Joe Mae Whitehead to become pastor. The dedication ceremony for the present church, located at 7770 Dale Avenue, was celebrated on August 24, 1984, with Rev. Timothy Hatter, pastor, officiating. (Courtesy of the Richmond Heights Historical Society Collection.)

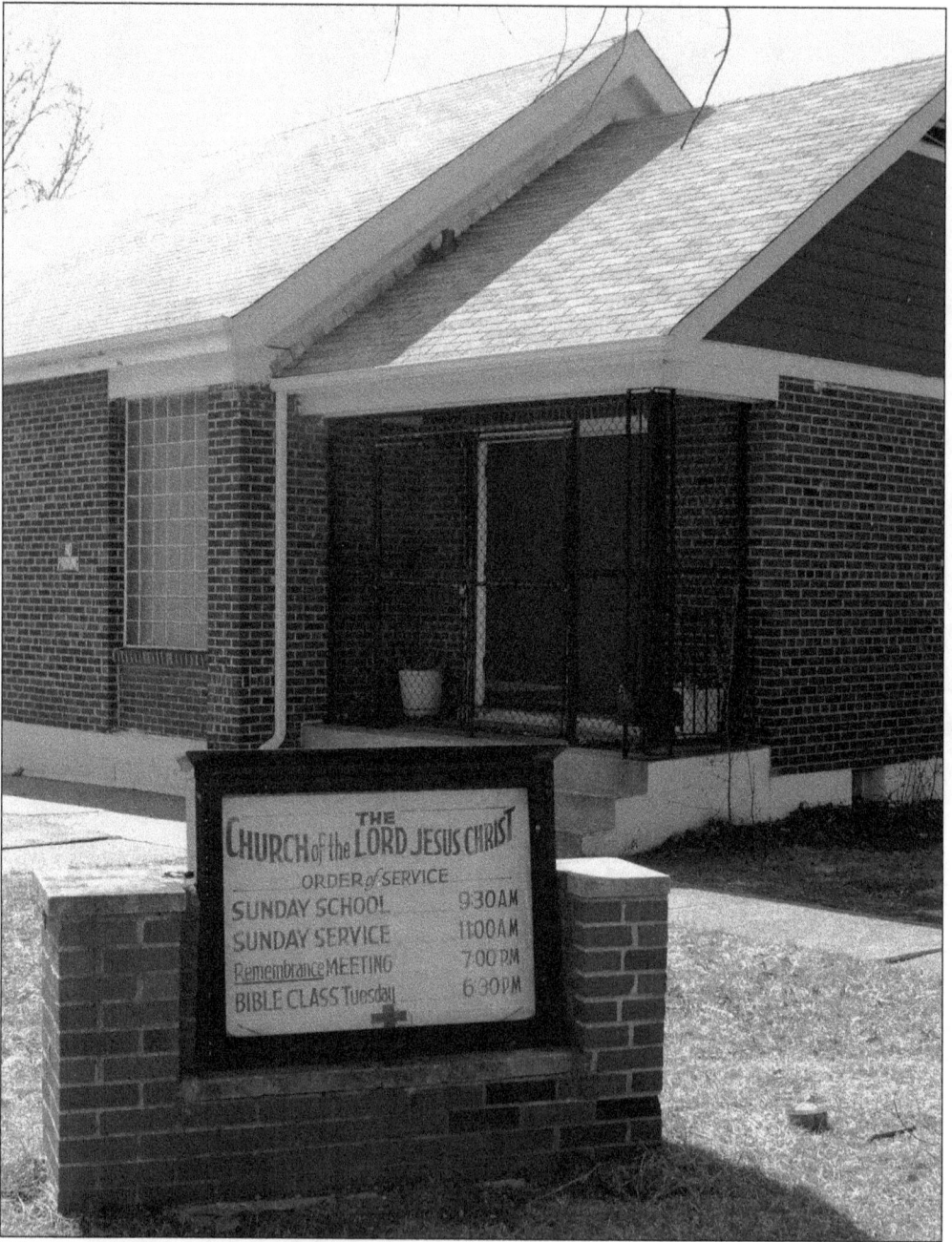

The Gospel Hall Church, or Church of the Lord Jesus Christ, stands at 7902 Dale Avenue. (Courtesy of the Richmond Heights Historical Society Collection.)

St. Mark's United Methodist Church

St. Mark's United Methodist Church was organized as a Sunday School on September 21, 1928 in the home of Mr. and Mrs. Andrew Williams, who lived in Richmond Heights. The first minister was the Reverend T.H. Parrish. Services were held in a rented church building until the congregation constructed their own church located at 8022 Dale Avenue.

St. Mark's was the only United Methodist Church in the Richmond Heights vicinity. It maintained an open door policy and members of the community were encouraged to join in worship services at all times. The congregation cooperated with other churches and social agencies in the community to render aid to the hungry, sick, and poor.

Unfortunately, there are no photographs of St. Mark's United Methodist Church in the Richmond Heights Historical Society Collection.

Servers Irv Rose (left) and Dick Krohr Jr. are shown at St. Luke the Evangelist Catholic Church. (Courtesy of the Richmond Heights Historical Society Collection.)

Four

SCHOOLS

Unique in St. Louis County, Richmond Heights has four school districts. The Maplewood-Richmond Heights School District lines extend east from the city of St. Louis, west along the south side of Wise Avenue, north to Clayton Road at Big Bend Boulevard, west on Clayton Road to Hanley Road, south on Hanley Road to West Bruno, and east along West Bruno to Bruno Avenue, and east again along Bruno Avenue back to the city of St. Louis. The Clayton School District runs along the north side of Wise Avenue to Big Bend Boulevard and north to Clayton Road, then east along Clayton Road to the city of St. Louis. The district lines pick up again on the west side of Hanley Road at Lake Forest, running west to Berkshire, with the southern boundary at Hanley Downs. Heading west from that subdivision, the boundary is Interstate 64. The Brentwood School District encompasses Hanley Downs, the former Manhassett Village, and the Chafford Woods subdivision. The Ladue School District includes residents in the Berkshire subdivision west to the east side of Lay Road, with a southern boundary of Interstate 64 and a northern boundary of Clayton Road.

By 1940, schools located within the city boundaries of Richmond Heights included: in the Maplewood-Richmond Heights District, the Richmond Heights School (later East Richmond, then Chaney) and the West Richmond School (later A. B. Green, then Chaney/A. B. Green); in the Clayton School District, Bellevue School and McMorrow School (both no longer standing); and two parochial schools, St. Luke the Evangelist School and Little Flower School. Another parochial school, Immacolata, opened after the time period covered by this book.

The Sutton School opened in 1906, elevating the number of elementary schools in the Maplewood School District to three, with Valley and Richmond Heights. (Courtesy of Andrew Rochman.)

The Richmond Heights School is pictured here in 1910. (Courtesy of the Richmond Heights Historical Society Collection.)

Miss Olsen's class poses at the Richmond Heights School in 1912. (Courtesy of the Richmond Heights Historical Society Collection.)

The West Richmond School, located at 1313 Boland Place, opened in 1917. It was sold by the school district in 2005. The building is set to reopen in 2006 as the Metropolitan School. (Courtesy of the Richmond Heights Historical Society Collection.)

The Chaney School opened on the grounds of what had been the East Richmond School (formerly Richmond Heights School). The name was changed to honor a longtime educator in the system, Oliver J. Chaney. This building was torn down in 2003 and replaced by the only elementary school in the Maplewood-Richmond Heights School District. (Courtesy of the Richmond Heights Historical Society Collection.)

The 1941 Maplewood-Richmond Heights High School graduation took place in the school's stadium. (Courtesy of Marion Buchroeder Gannon.)

OLD LINCOLN SCHOOL

Shown here is a drawing of the Old Lincoln School. Prior to 1911, African American students attended schools outside of Maplewood and Richmond Heights. One example was the Attacks School in Clayton. By 1911, the Maplewood School District (as it was then known) was renting rooms from Rev. Taylor in an African American church on Dale Avenue. The Lincoln School students were taught by Harvey Simms. The district purchased land across the street from the church on Dale Avenue as the student population grew. By 1932, the New Lincoln School had been built at 7917 Thomas Place to accommodate increasing numbers of students. Junior high students attended classes at the New Lincoln School instead of Lyndover because of segregation. For high school, black students traveled either to Douglas in Webster Groves or took long bus rides into the city of St. Louis to attend Sumner or Vashon. (Courtesy of Helen Abram.)

The New Lincoln School stood at 7917 Thomas Place. Closed by the school district in 1964, the building now serves as an assisted living facility called Richmond Terrace. (Courtesy of the Richmond Heights Historical Society Collection.)

Eighth-grade students at the New Lincoln School graduate in 1939. (Courtesy of Arthur Hinch.)

LINCOLN SCHOOL TEACHERS

HARVEY J. SIMMS	1909-1913	ELEASE (YOUNG) STRODE	1938-1963
LEE A. BOGGESS	1913-1916	LOUISE (LEWIS) DOUGLAS	1938-1962
MARTHA SHORES	1916-1920	ALBERTA (EVERETT) GANT	1938-1942
NETTIE HOWELL	1920-1934	NELLIE FRANCIS QUINN	1938-1939
THELMA JACKSON	1923-1929	CHARLESETTA (ALLMON) COLEMAN	1939-1964
JESSIE O. FIELDS	1924-1927	ELSIE (LAWTON) PLUMMER	1941-1943
IDA GOINS	1925-1927	CLOTHILDE MASON	1942-1943
HARRIET ASHCRAFT	1926-1931	VIRGINIA L. GLOVER	1942-1964
PORTIA PAYNE	1926-1930	MARGARET (HOGUE) BROWN	1943-1960
OBERA G. LOTHLEN	1928-1938	IRA B. BUTLER	1943-1960
V. WILLENE JACKSON	1929-1936	KATHRYN D. SMITH	1943-1944
MINEOLA JACKSON	1930-1936	KATIE TUGGLE	1943-1946
GRACE JAMES	1931-1934	MAXINE STARK	1944-1947
JULIA WALDEN	1931-1932	ELIZABETH N. YOUNGE	1947-1950
BERTHA M. (BLACK) RHODA	1932-1934	OLIVE (LONGDON) STINSON	1949-1964
EZRA TURNER	1934-1943	JOYCE (THOMPSON) SMITH	1950-1964
HAZEL (PARSONS) WALTON	1934-1946	FRANCES D. LEWIS	1951-1964
MARTHENIA (BATES) BONHAM	1934-1964	HELEH SCOGGINS	1956-1956
ARMSTEAD B. GREEN	1936-1961	JUNETTA SPURLING WHITE	1956-1957
EVANGELINE WOODS	1937-1942	FLOYD S. HEFLEY	1961-1964

Armstead B. Green, A Chronological Resume of the Lincoln School

This list, compiled by Armstead B. Green, records the Lincoln School teachers from 1909 to 1964.

Pictured here is the Bellevue School. (Courtesy of the Richmond Heights Historical Society Collection.)

A Mr. Scott worked as the maintenance man at the Bellevue School in 1927. (Courtesy of Sidney Freund.)

Vivian Hickel (left), Richard Nussbaum (center), and Sidney Freund attended eighth grade together at the Bellevue School in 1927. (Courtesy of Sidney Freund.)

The eighth-grade class at the Bellevue School poses for a photograph in 1927. (Courtesy of Sidney Freund.)

This undated photograph shows early teachers at St. Luke the Evangelist School. Pictured here are Sister Mary Ruth (left), Sister Mary Constanze (center), and Sister Mary Agatha, all members of the religious order of St. Joseph of Carondelet. (Courtesy of St. Luke the Evangelist Parish.)

FRONT: Genevieve Thomson Claire Forristall Marjorie Manahan Rev. J. A. McMahon Eugene White Anne Vernier Catherine Erman

MIDDLE: Francis McGinness Lawrence Riegel David Casey Eugene Liston Joseph Fischer Raymond Fagin Edward Thornton

TOP: George Almon James Cosgrove James Grutsch James Dowd Joseph Kenney Leo O'Leary Chares Gauchet

Members of the 1927 eighth-grade graduating class at St. Luke the Evangelist School pose with their pastor. Pictured here, from left to right, are the following: (first row) Genevieve Thomson, Claire Forristall, Marjorie Manahan, Rev. Joseph A. McMahon, Eugene White, Anne Vernier, and Catherine Erman; (second row) Francis McGinness, Lawrence Riegel, David Casey, Eugene Liston, Joseph Fischer, Raymond Fagin, and Edward Thornton; (third row) George Almon, James Cosgrove, James Grutsch, James Dowd, Joseph Kenney, Leo O'Leary, and Charles Gauchet. (Courtesy of St. Luke the Evangelist Parish.)

St. Luke the Evangelist Church and School had, in 1916, a combined building housing the original school of two rooms with four grades, and the church. In 1929, when the new church opened, the school building was converted into an eight-room facility with eight grades. (Courtesy of St. Luke the Evangelist Parish.)

St. Luke the Evangelist School is shown here in 1963. (Courtesy of the Richmond Heights Historical Society Collection.)

The first school at Little Flower was a two-room schoolhouse located on the corner of Boland Place and Arch Terrace, which opened in September 1926. Father Tammany arranged for the Dominican Sisters of Sparkhill, New York, to teach 50 students. The first teachers were Sister Georgiana, O.P., and Sister Louis, O.P. (Courtesy of Little Flower Parish.)

The present Little Flower School building, built in 1928, originally had two floors. The church took up the lower level, and the school and convent were situated on the second floor. The school opened in January 1929 with 150 students and five teaching sisters. The third floor, added in 1937, served as the school hall. (Courtesy of the Richmond Heights Historical Society Collection.)

The first eighth-grade class at Little Flower School graduated in June 1927. (Courtesy of Little Flower Parish.)

Five

PEOPLE AND PLACES

Richmond Heights retains a unique collection of architectural styles that illustrate the many facets of the community and its residents. One of the first homes was, of course, that associated with Frederick Niesen, erected in 1892 and described by those who knew it as a "white-pine mansion." As the community was developed during the early 1900s, many houses were constructed using lumber, brick, and other building materials gathered from the demolition following the epic fair at Forest Park. This was very common in St. Louis neighborhoods bordering the fair site, such as Richmond Heights. Brick was most commonly used in St. Louis city and county during the early 20th century. Abundant clay deposits made brick a practical and affordable material. In addition, it was "fireproof"—an extremely important factor, particularly after the great St. Louis fire of 1849.

Photographs of people often place them in relationship to their homes, a trend reflected in this chapter. Early single-family housing in Richmond Heights (pre-1920) illustrates the era in which it was built, with Victorian embellishments such as stained-glass windows and decorative frame and/or brickwork surrounding porches, roof lines, and windows. Homes constructed in the 1920s and 1930s most often reflect Craftsman and Tudor Revival influences. Richmond Heights also retains a large number of art deco–style apartments and businesses.

The city's legends surrounding its world's fair housing have perpetuated one of its most colorful tales: "The Forty Thieves," a nickname derived for 40 houses constructed in the neighborhood east of Big Bend Boulevard. Research indicates that many of these homes actually predate the world's fair. But as the story goes, local builder Walter Wilmot Reynolds gathered brick and lumber from the world's fair and erected the Forty Thieves using the salvaged (or stolen) fair remnants. Today, 38 of the original 40 houses survive. Each house is identical in plan: two stories in height, featuring (in most cases) a yellow brick facade (some are clad with stucco), and red brick rear and side exterior walls. Other identical features include primary doors, which are located off-center within the porch bay and bear a single oval light. The doors are offset by small individual windows with decorative brickwork above them. Reynolds's houses may not all be constructed with world's fair materials, yet their history is nearly as famous as the exposition itself, at least in Richmond Heights!

BEAUTIFUL MODERN HOMES ON MONTHLY PAYMENTS — $2,700.00 TO $3,950.
ARKET ST. CARS DIRECT TO PLACE, 5c FARE.   F. E. NIESEN, AGT. 10TH AND CHESTNUT

Seen here is a postcard view of Sunset Hill, Frederick Niesen's residential development. (Courtesy of the Richmond Heights Historical Society Collection.)

This vintage 1871 advertisement attempts to sell tracts which were formerly part of Rannells Farm. (Courtesy of Doug Houser.)

In 1906, Frederick Niesen built the Roney home at 32 Highland Terrace. (Courtesy of the Richmond Heights Historical Society Collection and Ann Roney Redman.)

$10 CASH AND
$10 PER MONTH

WILL BUY A
LOT FOR YOUR
OWN

HOME, SWEET HOME

IN———

South
Forest Park Hills

An Ideal Spot for a Home

SOUTH OF FOREST PARK, WEST OF McCAUSLAND AVE.

PRICES LOW

DAVID P. LEAHY HOUSE AND HOME CO.
800 CHESTNUT STREET

Home, Sweet Home. This sheet music advertisement showcases lots in the South Forest Park Hills area, being sold by the David P. Leahy House and Home Company. (Courtesy of Patricia Vilmer.)

The Frank and Mary DeBolt home, located at 1618 Bellevue Avenue, is pictured in 1908. At left, note the trestle, which spanned Arlington Avenue before Yale Avenue was created. (Courtesy of the Richmond Heights Historical Society Collection and Marie DeBolt.)

Dr. Russell Hill stands in front of his home at 1610 Bellevue Avenue in 1908. (Courtesy of the Richmond Heights Historical Society Collection.)

In 1903, this world's fair worker house was built at 7347 Wise Avenue. This was one of four identical homes, two of which were constructed to house fair workers. (Courtesy of the Richmond Heights Historical Society Collection.)

This 1907 photograph shows the house located at 7409 Wise Avenue, owned by the Carter Jones family at that time. (Courtesy of Ann Molasky Ibur and Janet Weber.)

In this streetscape are some of the Forty Thieves Homes on Lindbergh Drive. Following the 1904 St. Louis World's Fair, materials used for various fair buildings became available either for sale or for the taking, to anyone interested. According to legend, Walter Wilmot Reynolds used these materials to construct the near-identical houses known as the Forty Thieves Homes, which are all located east of Pennsylvania Avenue (Big Bend Boulevard). Reynolds, however, had begun building what would become 40 homes as early as 1898. Thus, he incorporated the salvaged material only into the homes built after 1904. (Courtesy of the Richmond Heights Historical Society Collection.)

Hampton Park is pictured here in 1911. (Courtesy of the Richmond Heights Historical Society Collection.)

Featured here is part of the entrance to Hampton Park. (Courtesy of the Richmond Heights Historical Society Collection.)

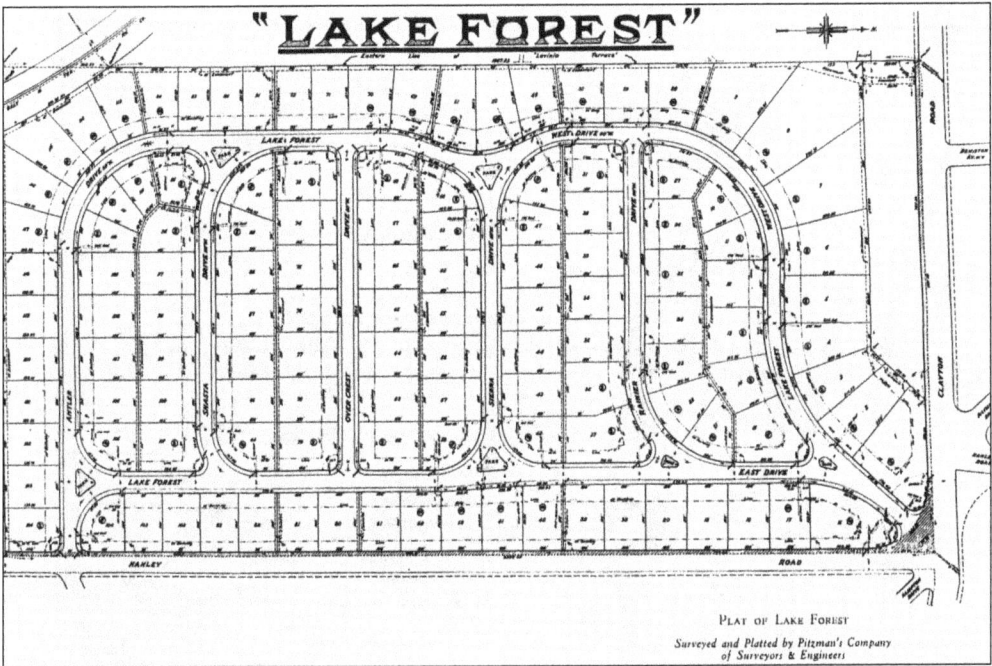

This plat map details the Lake Forest subdivision. (Courtesy of the Richmond Heights Historical Society Collection.)

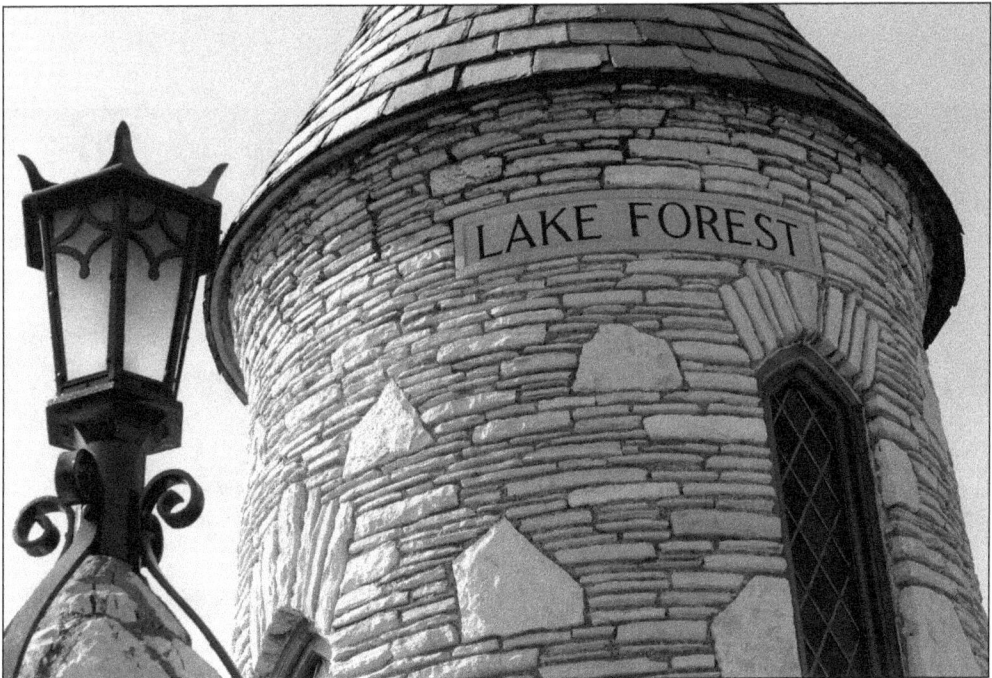

The entrance to Lake Forest is shown here. (Courtesy of the Richmond Heights Historical Society Collection.)

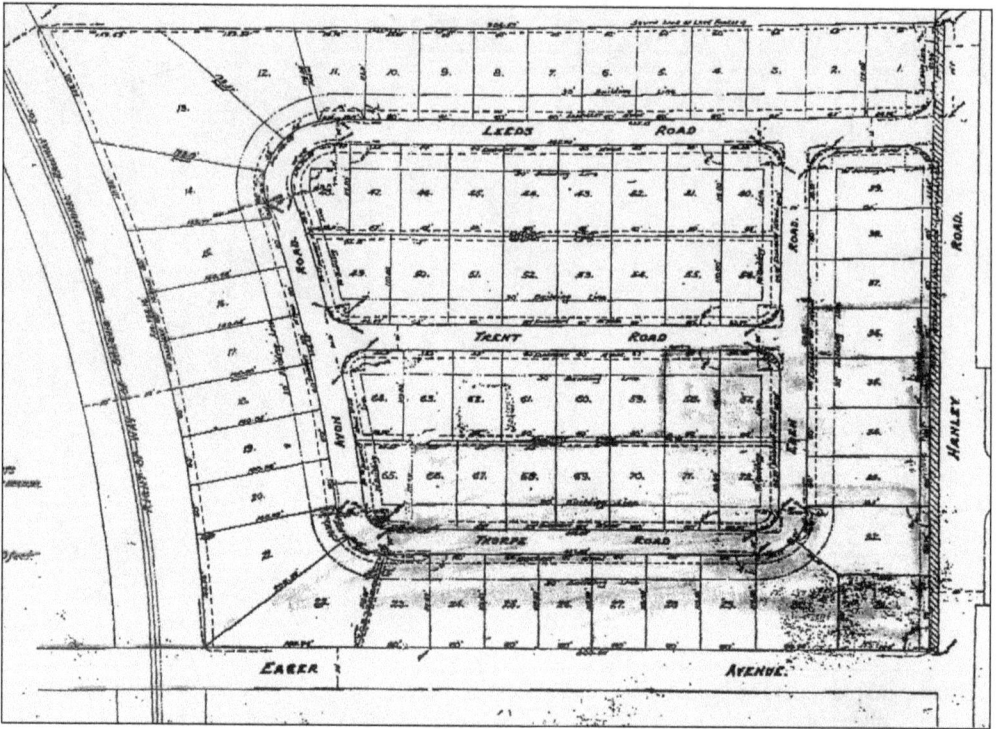

This plat map details the Hanley Downs subdivision. (Courtesy of the Richmond Heights Historical Society Collection.)

This is the northern end of the Hanley Downs subdivision, showing two of the first homes which were constructed in 1939–1940. Lake Forest borders the development further north. (Courtesy of Korinne Miller.)

Advertising promotes middle-class homes in Hanley Downs in 1940. Platted in 1938, Hanley Downs was designed by local architect Woodrow Kubatsky, the son of well-known German-trained architect Otto Kubatsky. Together with his wife, Rose Wichman Kubatsky, Woodrow developed this planned subdivision as a unique and affordable option for middle-class families and first-time homeowners. This type of development evolved from the City Beautiful movement of the late 19th and early 20th centuries. (Courtesy of Korinne Miller.)

Shown here is a Lavinia Gardens streetscape. Highway projects currently being scheduled by the Missouri Department of Transportation for the Interstate 170 and Interstate 40/64 interchange are set to raze some of the homes in this neighborhood. (Courtesy of the Richmond Heights Historical Society Collection.)

Virgil Wiesner stands in front of his family's Sears Catalogue home, located at 7435 Warner Avenue, in the early 1930s. (Courtesy of Virgil and Rosemary Wiesner.)

Joseph (center), Bernice, and Virgil
Wiesner pose in their side yard. (Courtesy
of Virgil and Rosemary Wiesner.)

Boyd Hogan (left) and Virgil Wiesner stand in the driveway of the Wiesner home in 1937.
(Courtesy of Virgil and Rosemary Wiesner.)

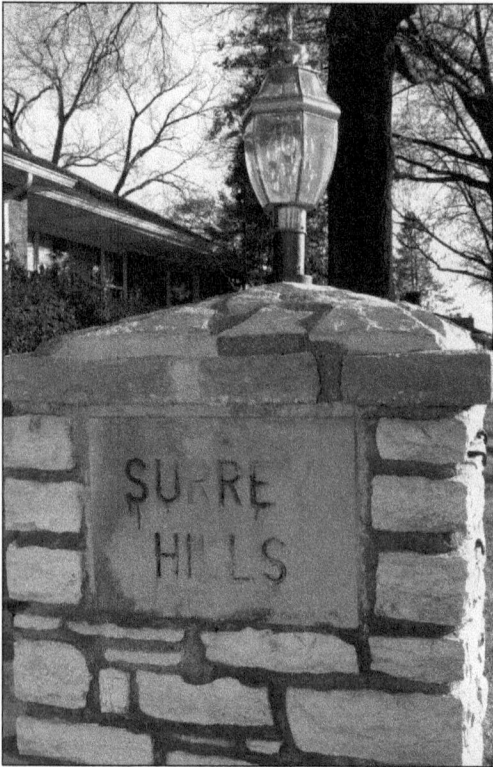

Seen here is the entrance to Surrey Hills. (Courtesy of the Richmond Heights Historical Society Collection.)

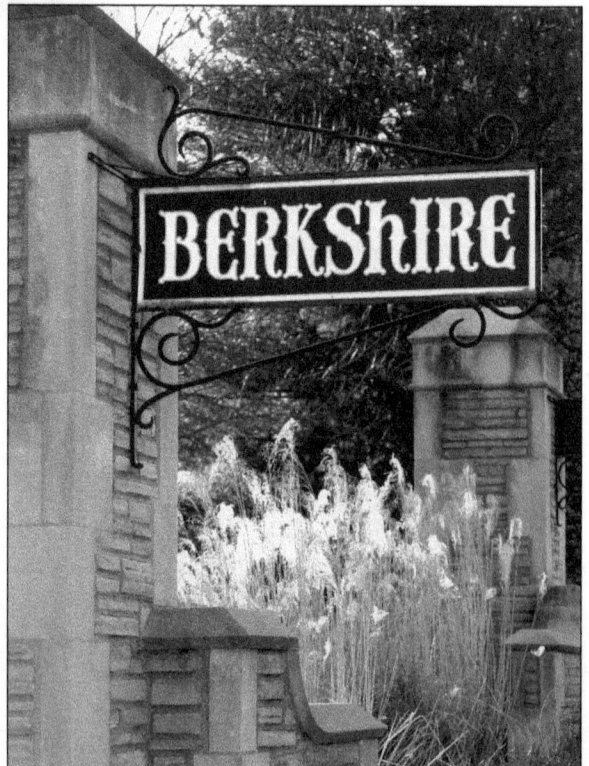

The entrance to Berkshire is pictured here. (Courtesy of the Richmond Heights Historical Society Collection.)

The land on which the private subdivision Ridgetop now sits was part of the property owned by Levi Wade and Lucy Childress (née Turner). Mr. Childress purchased 15 acres and the house, located at Clayton and McKnight Roads, in 1915. The development of the subdivision dates to 1926. Wade Childress and his wife, Josephine, lived at No. 17 Ridgetop from 1932 to 1939. By 1941, the subdivision included 32 residences. (Courtesy of the Richmond Heights Historical Society Collection.)

This art deco apartment building is situated at 1335 Highland Terrace. (Courtesy of the Richmond Heights Historical Society Collection.)

The Bellecourt Apartments (entrance pictured here) is listed on the National Register of Historic Places. (Courtesy of the Richmond Heights Historical Society Collection.)

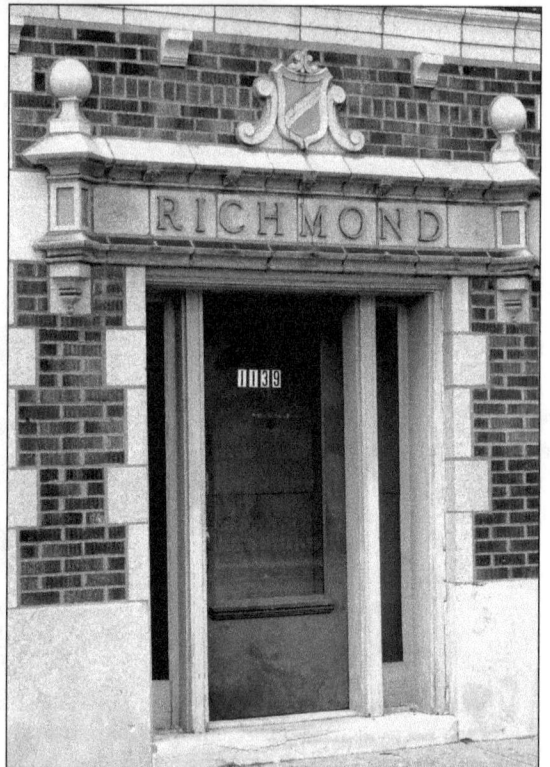

Shown here is the entrance to the Richmond Apartments at 1137–1145 Bellevue Avenue. (Courtesy of the Richmond Heights Historical Society Collection.)

This photograph shows the Bellevue Garden Apartments. (Courtesy of the Richmond Heights Historical Society Collection.)

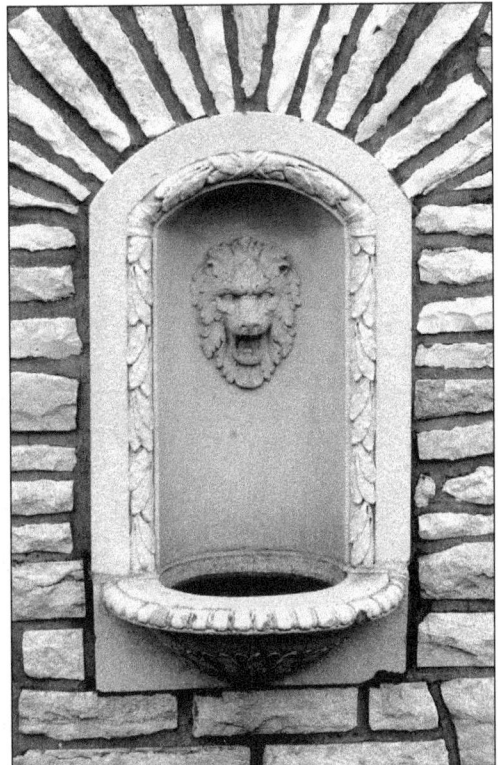

Featured on the left front corner of the Bellevue Garden Apartments is a ram's head water fountain. (Courtesy of the Richmond Heights Historical Society Collection.)

This stone sunburst marks the entrance to the Bellevue Garden Apartments. (Courtesy of the Richmond Heights Historical Society Collection.)

The apartment building at 1330–1338 Hawthorne Avenue showcases a lion's head water fountain on its primary edifice. (Courtesy of the Richmond Heights Historical Society Collection.)

Note the decorative art deco brickwork on the apartment building at 1330–1338 Hawthorne Avenue. (Courtesy of the Richmond Heights Historical Society Collection.)

Rose Terrace is located just north of Interstate 64, off Highland Terrace. (Courtesy of the Richmond Heights Historical Society Collection.)

Manhassett Village (entrance shown here) was demolished in 2005–2006 to prepare for a new condominium development. (Courtesy of the Richmond Heights Historical Society Collection.)

Pictured in 1962, the Manhassett Village complex was designed by Preston J. Bradshaw and constructed by H. B. Deal and Company in 1939. While it was not intended to provide low-cost housing, because the Federal Housing Authority insured the loan, rents ranged from $49 to $62 for three- to four-room apartments when the complex opened. (Courtesy of the Richmond Heights Historical Society Collection.)

Going, going, gone. What was once Manhassett Village is currently being developed as a condominium complex. (Courtesy of the Richmond Heights Historical Society Collection.)

Gone, but not forgotten. The Pedrotti house, once located at 7445 Ethel Avenue, was purchased by National Food Stores in 1984, along with all of the homes along the north side of the 7400 block of Ethel. This area is now commercial property known as Richmond Center. (Courtesy of Thelma Pedrotti.)

Six

BUSINESSES

Commercial properties in Richmond Heights were relatively few during the community's early years of development. For many years, the only stores in operation were Schulte's Market, located at 7537 Wise Avenue, and Riley's, located at 7425 Warner Avenue. The earliest commercial center appears to have been that of Bellevue Square, platted during the early 1920s. The original Bellevue Square commercial block remains in operation today, situated at the northwest corner of Bellevue and Wise Avenues. Additional early commercial strips developed along Dale Avenue, Big Bend Boulevard, Clayton Road, and Brentwood Boulevard. In 1946, only 19 of the city's 1,381 acres were in use for commercial and industrial interests, proving that commerce was not a major source of revenue for the city at that time. By the mid-1900s, more prominent business areas were appearing along Manchester Road in Maplewood and in St. Louis city, which border Richmond Heights to the south and east, respectively.

One reason that the city failed to develop a heavy commercial-use strip until the 1950s was due to its limited access to trolleys and streetcars. Although public transportation routes did reach the vicinity by the beginning of the 20th century, most were local in terms of their operation. The most famous of the city's streetcars was "the Dinky," a rural connection that was an extension loop of the Forest Park line, intended to provide service to West End Heights Amusement Park. It is clear that the city's earliest commercial strips were not constructed to directly serve the streetcar, although they were well within reach of public transportation. Instead, these early businesses were incorporated into the city to serve the residents of Richmond Heights. Streetcar passengers were much more likely to shop in downtown St. Louis or adjacent communities such as Maplewood, Kirkwood, and Webster Groves, all of which supported commercial strips intended to serve major streetcar lines.

Once the automobile became widely available and affordable to most Americans, Richmond Heights began to increase its commercial base. During this period, the city also expanded its residential developments, pushing its limits west into the newly formed neighborhoods of Hanley Downs, Lake Forest, and Hampton Park, designed during the 1920s and 1930s. Today, the residential character of Richmond Heights dominates the city's landscape, despite encroaching commercial development along Hanley Road and Brentwood Boulevard. Tucked away in older residential neighborhoods are small pockets that illustrate the city's early businesses, many of which remain in use today for commercial purposes.

Accoprding to Berl Katz and William J. Clouset, the Richmond Heights Dinky operated for only six years, from 1904 to 1910, along a route beginning on the Market line at Hi-Pointe, south on McCausland Avenue, west on Wise Avenue, south on North Avenue (now Yale Avenue), west on Park Avenue (now Dale Avenue), then southwest between Rankin Avenue and Hawthorne Avenue to Arlington Drive. Its abandonment coincided with the moving of the Market line's western terminal to Dale Avenue and Hawthorne Avenue. (Courtesy of the Richmond Heights Historical Society Collection.)

The West End Heights Amusement Resort existed from 1895 until it burned in 1913. It was located in the Hi-Pointe area at the terminus of the trolley lines. "Richmond Heights' first connection with St. Louis came in 1895, when the Lindell Railway's Chouteau Avenue electric street railway line reached the area known as Hi-Pointe. The first trolley to pass through Richmond Heights was the St. Louis & Kirkwood line," as documented by Berl Katz and William J. Clouset in 1963. (Courtesy of Andrew Rochman.)

The commercial area originally known as Bellevue Square is located at Bellevue and Wise Avenues. Today, it continues to offer a combination of commercial and apartment space. Advertisements in the Richmond Heights City and Business Directory of 1930 indicate that both Glaser Drug Company and Elmer Volkerding Dry Goods occupied this space at that time. (Courtesy of the Richmond Heights Historical Society Collection.)

Note the architectural detail on the commercial building at Bellevue and Wise Avenues. (Courtesy of the Richmond Heights Historical Society Collection.)

> "If You Don't Know Where to Go to Get What
> You Want, Go to Riley's"
>
> # Z. T. RILEY
>
> ## DEALER IN
>
> Electrical Supplies, Builders' Hardware,
> Pipe Fittings, Tools, Paints and Oil
>
> **HIland 5891** **7425 Warner Ave.**

This advertisement, originally printed in the Richmond Heights City and Business Directory of 1930, promotes the Z. T. Riley Hardware Store. The Zephaniah T. Riley family moved to Richmond Heights in 1910. The store operated out of the garage behind the family home at 7425 Warner Avenue. It remained at that location until 1954, when Leonard Riley moved it to 1605 Big Bend Boulevard.

The Park Avenue Post Office was situated on Oakland Avenue at Yale Avenue. Many residents came to this facility to pick up their mail before home delivery was widely available. (Courtesy of the Richmond Height Historical Society Collection.)

Located at the intersection of Clayton Road and Big Bend Boulevard, this corner building is typical of the combination retail and apartment space throughout the older sections of Richmond Heights. Among early occupants were Glaser Drug Store and Piggly Wiggly. (Courtesy of the Richmond Heights Historical Society Collection.)

This commercial-apartment building stands at the southwest corner of Ethel Avenue and Big Bend Boulevard. The Richmond Heights City and Business Directory of 1930 listed the following businesses in the 1000 block of Big Bend Boulevard: M&M Auto Service, Kempland Realty, Norman's Beauty Shop, Westmoor Hardware, Rasmussen Realty, Heckman's Bakery, Overhead Door, Vickery Bricklaying, and O. E. Miller Plumbing. (Courtesy of the Richmond Heights Historical Society Collection.)

The Dale Avenue section of the business area was served by the Dinky in the early 1900s. Here, again, is the combination retail and apartment space seen elsewhere. Among the businesses that have served the community from this location are New Dale Market, Wallar's Drug Store, Ryan's Groceries and Meats, and Joe's Shoe Repair. (Courtesy of the Richmond Heights Historical Society Collection.)

Pictured here is another combination commercial space and apartment building featuring art deco architectural details, located at Hawthorne and Dale Avenues. This corner has housed markets, cafeterias, bars, and architectural firms, among other enterprises, during the course of its history. (Courtesy of the Richmond Heights Historical Society Collection.)

This postcard of St. Mary's Hospital, which was designed by Albert B. Groves in 1923, was issued at the time of the hospital's formal dedication on June 10, 1924. The board of alderman granted approval for the building in 1922. The 18-acre tract had previously housed Campbell's Forest Home, a notorious gambling resort and roadhouse, which mysteriously burned to the ground. The city annexed this area in 1919 and acted quickly after the fire to grant approval to the Franciscan Sisters of Mary to build their hospital. (Courtesy of the Richmond Heights Historical Society Collection and Marie DeBolt.)

Behind St. Mary's Hospital, the Franciscan Sisters of Mary built their convent. This photograph was taken in 1924, shortly after completion. Nearby residents recalled seeing the young nuns roller skating around the grounds. (Courtesy of the Richmond Heights Historical Society Collection.)

This 1920s aerial photograph shows the community surrounding St. Mary's Hospital. To the south is the former Niesen family compound, the Niesen residential development at Sunset Hill, and the cable track to Wise Avenue are all visible. (Courtesy of the Richmond Heights Historical Society Collection.)

St. Mary's Medical Center, part of the Sisters of St. Mary Healthcare System, is seen here as it appears today. (Courtesy of the Richmond Heights Historical Society Collection.)

This Mobil gas station was located in an island at Clayton Road and Big Bend Boulevard. The pyramid-shaped light at the top of the tower was purportedly used as a navigation aid for pilots flying to Lambert Field. (Courtesy of Andrew Rochman.)

In the late 1950s, a fire destroyed the Mobil station. It was rebuilt and remains a Mobil station to this day. (Courtesy of the Richmond Heights Historical Society Collection.)

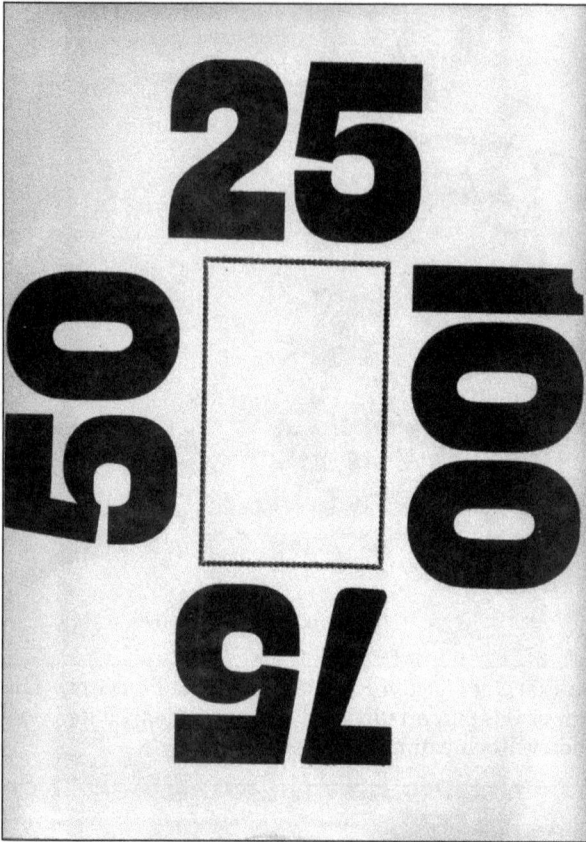

An ice card was displayed in the front window of a home, with the number of pounds needed at the top, to let the ice man know what he should deliver. When the delivery was made, the ice man brought a block of ice into the kitchen and placed it directly in the ice box. (Courtesy of the Richmond Heights Historical Society Collection and Marion Gannon.)

This advertisement for Young Ice and Coal appeared in the Richmond Heights City and Business Directory of 1930. (Courtesy of the Richmond Heights Historical Society Collection.)

The Crossroads Restaurant was located on the south side of Clayton Road, near the intersection where Brentwood Boulevard crossed Clayton Road. (Courtesy of the Richmond Heights Historical Society Collection.)

Another popular restaurant, the Turnpike, stood on the east side of Big Bend Boulevard, near Clayton Road. (Courtesy of Andrew Rochman.)

The Esquire Theatre opened with great fanfare in 1939. It was one of a series of theaters designed by Robert Boller. While the building has been expanded and renovated, it still remains an excellent example of art deco architecture. (Courtesy of the Richmond Heights Historical Society Collection.)

From 1939 to 1959, the Esquire Bowling Alley was located on the second floor at 6710 Clayton Road, over a Woolworth's five-and-ten. The 20-lane alley was open seven days a week, and the pin boys lived in the building. In 1988, Lorraine Butler remembered, "After bowlers finished their games, they would come in the snack bar to eat, drink, play records, and oftentimes to dance." (Courtesy of the Richmond Heights Historical Society Collection.)

Pictured here is the Esquire Theatre sign, as it looks today. (Courtesy of the Richmond Heights Historical Society Collection.)

Policy

1939

Esquire THEATRE of TOMORROW
Clayton Rd., at Big Bend—Phone, STerling 3300

DOORS OPEN

TIME SCHEDULE

Daily at ....6:30 P. M.
Saturday at ....1:30 P. M.
Sunday and
Holidays at ....1:00 P. M.

★ ★ ★ ★ ★ ★

ADMISSION

Evenings and Sunday
After 2:00 P. M.

POPULAR PRICES

Adults 35c
Children 10c

Saturday Till 6:00 P. M.
Sundays and
Holidays Till 2:00 P. M.

Adults 25c
Children 10c

All Prices Plux Tax

THE ARISTOCRAT
ESQUIRE
OF ENTERTAINMENT

Complete change of program every Thursday. Continuous shows Saturday, Sunday and Holidays. Full complete show at all times begins at 9:00 P. M.

Esquire PERSONNEL

Harry Greenman ....Director
Eugene Baker...............Public Relations
W. C. Persons..................Photography
Louis J. Kemp..................Advertising
Bernice Grommet...............Art Director
Jimmie Downey............Musical Director
Marjorie Weber.....................Cashier
Allen Hatfield...............Door Supervisor
Hiram Neuwoelmer, Jr..........Receptionist
Harold Kessler ....Receptionist
Hugh MacLean ....Superintendent
Joseph J. Schrempp............Projectionist
Roscoe Hawkins ....Projectionist
George Bierman ....Maintenance

COURTEOUS *Esquire* STAFF

M. Fairhead
B. Frehlich
M. Gibstein
D. Greenman
J. Grodsky
P. Julian
J. Kramer
G. Mahe
W. Reynolds
B. Stearn
F. Smith
L. Smith
M. Barker
E. Bartsch
P. Baum
F. Woolf
A. Marcheto

This image was taken from the Esquire 50th anniversary booklet. This policy page lists schedules, prices, and theater personnel in 1939. (Courtesy of the Richmond Heights Historical Society Collection.)

The Esquire staff pose on the main stage of the theater in 1939, as shown in the Esquire 50th anniversary booklet. (Courtesy of the Richmond Heights Historical Society Collection.)

The building at 1200 South Big Bend Boulevard was constructed in 1936 for Dr. Samuel A. Bassett. The property is an early example of the International style, designed by architect Edouard J. Mutrux. Mutrux received his degree from Washington University and later started an architectural firm with William Adair Bernoudy, who studied architecture under Frank Lloyd Wright. Bassett and his partner, Dr. Thomas A. Coates, occupied the building until 1962. It remains in use today as a law firm and is listed on the National Register of Historic Places. (Courtesy of the Richmond Heights Historical Society Collection.)

Seven

African American Community

Redevelopment of Richmond Heights's historic African American community is set to occur in 2006–2007. While much of the black community favored this change, it is fortunate Heine and Croghan Architects have committed to retaining a small triangular section of the neighborhood, as requested by a majority of the city council. This will preserve a remnant of the neighborhood. Because much of this history will be lost, this entire chapter is dedicated to the African American community of Richmond Heights.

This historic section of the city owes its very existence to Evens and Howard Fire Brick Company. In the early 1900s, segregation restricted African Americans to small enclaves in St. Louis City and County. It took a company with political clout to gain approval from St. Louis County officials to develop neighborhoods in Brentwood and Richmond Heights for black families. The company needed workers for its brickworks nearby. Once it began to build housing for its employees, other African American families soon moved to Richmond Heights.

In this chapter, Edna Miller Taylor invites readers to share memories of her family and the closely knit surrounding community. Families grew their own vegetables and fruits, raised chickens, made their own clothes, and shopped only for what they could not produce. Lorraine Johnson, another longtime resident, recalled, "For recreation—we made our own—sometimes our recreation and helping to put food on the table were one and the same. We would go berry picking, and we would go nutting in the fall."

Arthur Hinch, a childhood resident, provided a wonderful story about playing ball in a field across Hanley Road. While the ball diamond was exclusively for adults on weekends, the boys were allowed to play there during the week. There were acres of corn, tomatoes, melons, and other crops growing around the periphery of this field, a delicious temptation for a boy, who just happened to play center field. He prayed for a hard-hit ball so that he could run into the tomato patch and start eating. While his teammates kept yelling, "Where's the ball?" he acted like he could not find it until he was ready to come out.

Two Evens and Howard Fire Brick Company advertisements appeared in the Richmond Heights City and Business Directory of 1930. The history of this business is closely intertwined with that of the early African American residents of the city. (Courtesy of the Richmond Heights Historical Society Collection.)

Located at 8121 Hicks Avenue, this house is the only unaltered example of the type of housing Evens and Howard Fire Brick built for its workers in Richmond Heights. These houses, called two-by-twos, provided two families accommodations with three rooms each. The original structures did not include basements. (Courtesy of the Richmond Heights Historical Society Collection.)

This earlier view of Hicks Avenue looks west from Laclede Station Road. (Courtesy of the Richmond Heights Historical Society Collection.)

This streetscape of Hicks Avenue looks east from Hanley Road. The only remaining Evens and Howard Brick worker homes are located in the 8000 and 8100 blocks of Hicks Avenue. (Courtesy of the Richmond Heights Historical Society Collection.)

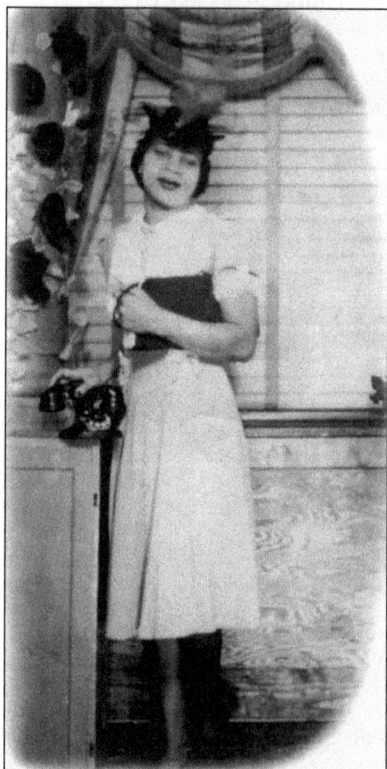

Mary Watson was born in Richmond Heights on May 23, 1917. She married George T. Watson in 1937, and they raised their children—Georgia, Juanita, Clinton "Kenny," and Sharon—in this community. Mary was active in the Church of the Living God. Besides caring for her family, she worked as a school bus driver, caretaker of children, maid and cook, and healthcare provider. She died on April 9, 2005. (Permission obtained from Georgia Watson Crenshaw.)

James E. Fiddmont and Lucy Barnett were married in Arkansas in 1918. They moved to St. Louis in 1921 and eventually settled on Maplewood's West Bruno Avenue, which is on the Richmond Heights boundary. There were 12 Fiddmont children: Jack William, Lavern, Robert, Vera Mae, Nina Vernita, James Elbert Jr., Frederick Charles, Doris Arlene, Grace Darling, Haarlan Day, Charles Ballard, and Norman Samuel. Rev. James E. Fiddmont Sr. served as pastor at Mount Zion Missionary Baptist Church for 32 years and was active in the community as well. (Permission obtained from Frederick Fiddmont.)

Robert Abram stands on the east side of Hanley Road near Alabama Avenue in this undated photograph. To the left and behind Abram is the building which served as the first home of the Mount Zion Missionary Baptist Church. Services were held in the basement. To the right is Will Chaney's Restaurant and Store. (Courtesy of Lillie Mae Warner.)

Iniss Warner poses with her godmother, Inez Miller, in front of a two-family flat on Hanley Road. In the 1950s, the building was demolished for the Daniel Boone Expressway (Interstate 64). (Courtesy of Lillie Mae Warner.)

This house, located at 1711 Banneker in the historic African American section of Richmond Heights, is set to be torn down in 2006–2007. (Courtesy of the Richmond Heights Historical Society Collection.)

This house formerly stood at 8000 Elinore. One of the unique features of this property was the stone wall that marked the front entrance. (Courtesy of the Richmond Heights Historical Society Collection.)

Legendary jazz singer Mae Wheeler is pictured here in a recent photograph. (Courtesy of Mae Wheeler.)

Situated at 1751 Laclede Station Road, this house was designed for Dr. Henry E. Hampton by Harris Armstrong in 1941. Armstrong also designed two of Dr. Hampton's office buildings. The doctor was a highly respected African American physician and surgeon. He served as the first medical director at Homer G. Phillips Hospital from 1937 to 1941. Dr. Hampton raised his family in Richmond Heights. His son Henry Hampton Jr. became an award-winning filmmaker perhaps best known for his documentary series on the civil rights movement, *Eyes on the Prize*. Washington University established the Henry Hampton Collection as part of its film and media archive following his early death in 1998. (Courtesy of the Richmond Heights Historical Society Collection.)

Thomas Rusan Sr. married Mildred Vivens, who grew up in Richmond Heights. After their marriage, the Rusans lived on Argus Place, where they raised their three children: Julia, Thomas Jr., and Marian. The Rusan children attended Lincoln School, but because of segregation, commuted by bus (three transfers) to Sumner High School in St. Louis city. All three Rusan children graduated from college. Thomas Jr. studied medicine at Meharry Medical School and settled in Richmond Heights with his wife, Georgia Talleur Rusan, where they lived first on Argus Place and then on Laclede Station Road in two different locations until the Rusans developed a neighborhood for black professionals in the Clayton Park Addition and built their home on Bennett Avenue. Dr. Rusan was a prominent physician with a private practice in St. Louis county and was a member of the staff at Homer G. Phillips Hospital. The senior Rusans were very active in the Richmond Heights community, involving themselves in projects ranging from working to improve the roads in the African American neighborhood, to getting out the vote in 1945 to defeat an attempt to take homes in their community for a city park. (Permission obtained from Georgia Rusan.)

Adapted from *Growing Up in Richmond Heights*, by Edna Miller Taylor

In 1913 the year Richmond Heights became incorporated, Samuel Miller, Sr. and Mary Virginia (Bell) Miller moved their family from an area in St. Louis City called Petersville to Argus Place. Along with the Millers came Mrs. Miller's mother, Mary Elizabeth (Rice) Bell, who bought the house next door to them.

In the early years, Argus Place had no electricity, running water, or indoor plumbing. People used kerosene lamps to light their homes. Water was carried into the homes from the few wells nearby, or purchased from a vendor. Homes were heated by iron stoves which burned coal and wood.

The Evens & Howard Brick Works was a company which owned a brickyard and a clay mine located in Brentwood. The company needed to entice workers to come live and work in "the country," so they began building built bungalows and roads in Brentwood and Richmond Heights beginning in 1906, near their factory. The roads were packed hard with a combination of dirt and rocks, and when it rained, they became muddy and almost impossible to travel. The homes were all the same featuring frame structures with three rooms and a front porch, and no basements. It was into one of these bungalows that the Miller family moved.

Edna Miller was born in her parent's home on Argus Place in 1927. She was the youngest of eight children. Even before she was born, changes were made to the family home introducing improvements like electricity and running water. When a basement was added (by digging under the house), so was a coal furnace. The Millers needed to be creative about using space with such a large family. One way they did this was to put their kitchen in the basement. As Edna remembered, "For a brief while there were no stairs leading from upstairs down to the basement. In order to get to the kitchen, we had to leave by the front or rear door and go around to the back of the house to enter the basement. This proved to be most inconvenient at times, especially if you got thirsty during the night for a drink of water."

Edna recalled, "My dad had a huge garden which seemed to stretch at least a block long. He would plant almost every vegetable you can think of...Sometimes my dad would allow my brother and me to help with the hoeing and watering of the small plants and, of course, we all took part in picking the vegetables when they were ready." Mr. Miller produced enough to share with relatives in St. Louis City and many neighbors and friends. According to Edna, "Dad's garden was located north of Harter Avenue. which ran east and west for some distance ending at the Hampton Creek. At the back of the garden was a fresh spring from which we watered the young plants. Since it was free flowing, we also used it to cool our faces and soak our feet, and yes, we drank the cool, fresh spring water too."

One day, Edna's father made her a swing,

...he picked up a long, thick rope and took me by the hand, walking down Harter and across the bridge at Hampton Creek...I was wondering all the time what he planned to do with that rope. He stood for a time in the shade looking at all the huge tall trees. He put his hands on his hips and walked around, and I did the same. Finally he seemed to have made up his mind about something. He looked around until he found a fair sized rock which he tied the rope around. Then he tossed the rock with the rope attached over a huge limb...he found what he was looking for - an old tire. He rolled the tire back to where the rope was hanging and tied the rope around the tire several times. He took the other end of the rope and tied it around the trunk of the tree. He had made me a tire swing."

Edna lived most of her life in Richmond Heights. She worked for the city in the maintenance and building departments for many years, and was active in the community. She died in December, 1989.

These are some memories from Richmond Heights resident Edna Miller Taylor.

Eight

COMMUNITY

Citizen involvement in the community was demonstrated by the earliest residents and continues today. The historical society's collection documents some poignant examples. From volunteering to dig trenches and install sewer lines, to sending sons to war and then memorializing those who died; from providing leaders and opportunities through boy scouting, to serving as volunteer firefighters, the people of Richmond Heights have willingly participated and thereby created a strong and vibrant place in which to live.

The community's loss of six young soldiers in World War I is better understood through Mildred Rice's words describing the war's impact: "Richmond Heights sent 70 sons. Nine of these had been or were members of the Richmond Heights Presbyterian Church or Sunday School. . . . Gold stars on our church flag honor two who died: Roy Lile and Walter Rupert. A monument erected at Arlington and Bellevue Avenues was dedicated to the 70 boys on Memorial Day of 1923." The sacrifices are better realized by knowing that two of the mothers, pictured on page 114 with the Red Cross Women's Auxiliary, will lose their sons in the war: Mrs. Winzenberg and Mrs. Gray.

In 1988, Thelma Pedrotti gathered local memories for a booklet entitled *Down Memory Lane*. In this collection, sisters Mae Gannon and Dorothy Hartman share their stories of life at 7307 Hoover Avenue, the home that their parents, James and Bridget Brennan, built in 1909. The following is an excerpt:

> The Brennans had chickens, pigs, a prized rooster and a prized sow. . . . The streets were mud. The Brennans had two telephones—a Kinloch and a Bell. They had indoor plumbing; others on the block did not. . . . When shades went down in the kitchen on Saturday night . . . it was bath time.
>
> Everyone shopped at Schulte's Grocery Store at Wise and Highland Terrace or George Collins' Grocery. Other goods were bought from peddlers . . . the produce man, the ice man and the rag man. . . . The Hi-Pointe Theater has been there since we were kids. Hartman's Bakery was on McCausland down from the theater. Cheshire was originally a root beer stand. When they added hamburgers, the name became Medart's. It was a treat to get a Medart's hamburger . . .
>
> . . . For entertainment, you played in the street with the kids on your block. You roller skated . . . played on stilts, or played ball. Not too many kids had bikes. The only swimming pool was at Forest Park Highlands. . . . In winter, everyone skated at Forest Park. They would have big bonfires. It was also a treat to sleigh ride down Ethel from Bellevue to Big Bend.

Volunteers dig trenches and install pipe for sewers on Arlington Avenue in 1912. Pictured here, from left to right, are James L. Brown, Richard Krohr, Fred Kuchenbuch, Ed Buehning, hired man August ?, Gerald McAtee, Mr. Sweet, Frank DeBolt Sr., and Jacob E. Lintzenich. (Courtesy of the Richmond Heights Historical Society Collection and Marie DeBolt.)

This second photograph reveals additional volunteers who built the Arlington Avenue sewer system. Numbered one to five are Frank Stone, Ralph McGaghey, Gerald McAtee, Jim Cahill, and Walter Buehning. Number six is Archie Biggs. Numbers 7 to 12 are John Weipert, Raymond Herr, Glen McAtee, Oliver Cahill, Frank DeBolt Jr., and John C. DeBolt. (Courtesy of the Richmond Heights Historical Society Collection and Marie DeBolt.)

Pvt. Walter M. Rupert died at Camp
Meade, Maryland, in 1918. (Courtesy of
the Richmond Heights Historical Society
Collection and Marie DeBolt.)

Claude Hutchinson appears in front
of a group of soldiers at Quantico,
Virginia, in September 1917. He grew
up on Francis Place in Richmond
Heights. (Courtesy of Jo Ann Smith.)

These women hosted a benefit on the Niesen lot for the Richmond Heights Red Cross Community Shop on June 22, 1918. The names on the back of the original print, from left to right, are as follows: (first row) Mrs. McKinley, Mrs. F. D. DeBolt Sr., Mrs. E. Gissler, Mrs. F. Stillman, unidentified, Mrs. Joseph Markham, unidentified, Miss Schwatzen, Miss Schwatzen, Mrs. Walter Craig, and Mrs. Hervey; (second row) Mrs. B. B. Custer, Mrs. Lintzenich, Mrs. Stevens, Mrs. D. M. Hazlett, four unidentified, Mrs. Fred Kuchenbuch, unidentified, Mrs. Francis Thornton, Mrs. Raymond Grutsch, Mrs. Galbraith, Mrs. Unger, Mrs. Kurtz, Miss Estelle Kennedy, Mrs. Kennedy, two unidentified, and Mrs. Mutchler; (third row) Mrs. Robert Hughes, unidentified, Mrs. Winzenberg, Mrs. Robert Ries, unidentified, Mrs. Russell S. Hill, Mrs. Kanur, Mrs. Jefferies, unidentified, Miss Wischer, Mrs. Grey, unidentified, Mrs. Fred Kraemer, Mrs. John Hoffman, unidentified, and Mrs. Fred Keene. (Courtesy of the Richmond Heights Historical Society Collection and Marie DeBolt.)

This memorial card recognizes the contribution made by Mary DeBolt in establishing a World War I memorial for those men who died as a result of service: Lee Goff, Charles Gray, Roy Lile, Manuel Johnson, Walter Rupert, and Roy Winzenberg. (Courtesy of the Richmond Heights Historical Society Collection and Marie DeBolt.)

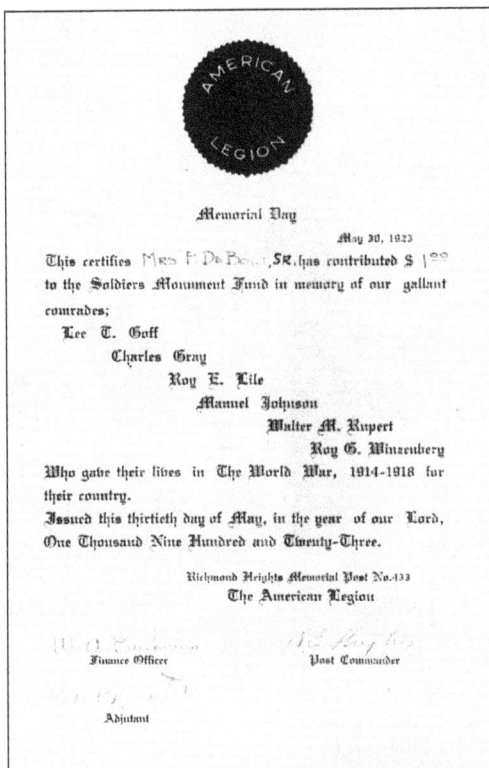

Memorial Day

May 30, 1923

This certifies Mrs F. DeBolt, SR. has contributed $ 1.00 to the Soldiers Monument Fund in memory of our gallant comrades;

Lee T. Goff

Charles Gray

Roy E. Lile

Manuel Johnson

Walter M. Rupert

Roy G. Winzenberg

Who gave their lives in The World War, 1914-1918 for their country.

Issued this thirtieth day of May, in the year of our Lord, One Thousand Nine Hundred and Twenty-Three.

Richmond Heights Memorial Post No. 133
The American Legion

Finance Officer   Post Commander

Adjutant

At Bellevue and Arlington Avenues, this World War I canon stood as a memorial to the Richmond Heights men who served during the war. The canon was dismantled and donated to the war effort during World War II. A canon from that war was mounted in the same location. The plaque from the first monument can now be seen in front of the Odie J. Wilkinson Veterans of Foreign War Post 3500, located at 1717 Big Bend Boulevard. (Courtesy of the Richmond Heights Historical Society Collection.)

Boy Scouts swim in the Big River in Allenton, Missouri, in 1918. Pictured from left to right are John Ehrman, Frank McDonald, Frank DeBolt, Harry Keene, and Ferdinand Weinert. (Courtesy of the Richmond Heights Historical Society Collection and Marie DeBolt.)

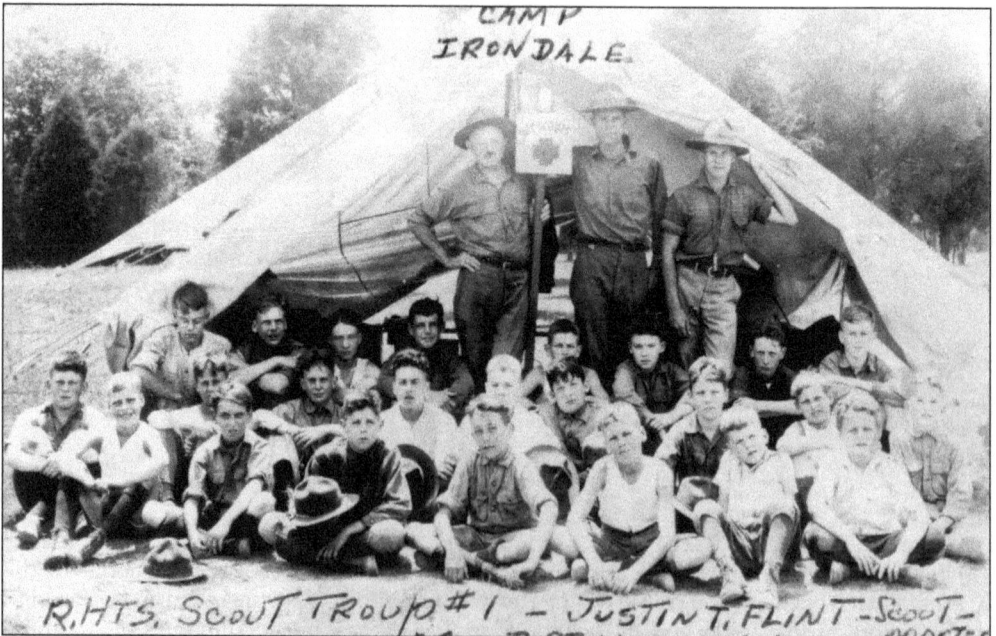

Richmond Heights Boy Scout Troop No. 1 members are shown with scout master Justin Flint at Camp Irondale in 1918. (Courtesy of the Richmond Heights Historical Society Collection and Marie DeBolt.)

Members of Richmond Heights Boy Scout Troop No. 1 attend Camp Roosevelt in 1919. Justin Flint serves as scout master. (Courtesy of the Richmond Heights Historical Society Collection and Marie DeBolt.)

Cub Scout Pack 38 celebrates its first birthday on March 8, 1939. Pictured here, from left to right, are the following: (first row) George Sauter, Robert Brendecki, Raymond Gallaher, Charles Austin, Billy Bohres, Mac Owen Gillaspy, and Billy Shillig; (second row) Jack Wrape, Jack Thye, Benny Best, Benny McKnight, James Bordgett, Billie Lubeski, and Eddie Windsor; (third row) Jerry Mitchell, Frank Garner, Nelson Clark Jr., Dick Verser, Billy Klosterman, Dicky Abel, Buddy Brown, and Alfred Rogers; (fourth row) Dick Reed, Toby Grone, and Roger Larson; (fifth row) Pete Norvell, Elmer Brown, Alfred Larson, Frank Bubee, Jimmy Coombs, Nelson Clark Sr., Jack Stochl, Aaron Gorman, and John Barnard. (Courtesy of the Richmond Heights Historical Society, Nelson Clark Special Collection).

Susie's Kitchen Band members in the early 1920s included, from left to right, Mrs. Joe Bante, Eva Krohr, Tillie Thompson, Marie Schultze, Ag Riley, Mrs. Frankman, Mrs. Clem Arrl, and Gert Bank. (Courtesy of St. Luke the Evangelist Parish.)

Taken from the roof of the Niesen home, this 1927 view looks south. (Courtesy of Christine O'Shaughnessy.)

This 1929 view looks west along Wise Avenue to Bellevue. (Courtesy of the Richmond Heights Historical Society Collection.)

The year of the big fire at Yale Avenue and Clayton Road is disputed. Robert Kuhn, who lived at 1009 Yale Avenue at the time, believes the fire occurred before 1939, perhaps in 1937 or 1938. He describes a three-story building owned by Charles Curry, in which there were 18 to 24 apartments in the upper floors and a variety of commercial enterprises on the ground floor. Kuhn recalls the businesses being Park Savings and Trust, the Midland Liquor Store, Jack Ray the jeweler, and a catering company owned by Tony Fracchia. The third floor of the building could never be restored. Betty Nast Notter, however, thinks the fire occurred in 1939 or 1940. She remembers the blaze burned for a whole week. Her father, Frederick Nast, was a volunteer firefighter who would come home from work and immediately go to help out. Both Clayton Road and Yale Avenue were closed in the area of the fire for a week. The Forest Park streetcar had to stop at Hi-Pointe because of this. Miraculously, no one was seriously hurt.(Courtesy of the Richmond Heights Historical Society Collection.)

This 1931 view of Eager Road looks east to the Kirkwood-Ferguson track. (Courtesy of the Richmond Heights Historical Society Collection.)

Civil Works Administration workers dig a trench for the Snowden Avenue sewer line during the 1930s. (Courtesy of the Richmond Heights Historical Society Collection.)

Here are additional views of workers with the Civil Works Administration creating the Snowden Avenue sewer line in the 1930s. (Courtesy of the Richmond Heights Historical Society Collection.)

This early-1950s aerial photograph shows the area where the Daniel Boone Expressway (now Interstate 40/64) would raze homes. On the left, in a vacant lot, is the former location of the Niesen family compound. On the right is the back of the Franciscan Sisters of Mary convent on the grounds of St. Mary's Hospital. During construction of the interstate, Harter Avenue was completely eliminated up to Big Bend Boulevard. One side of Harter west of Big Bend (the 7500 block) was left to overlook the highway, and from Claytonia Terrace west, the rest of Harter was taken. (Courtesy of the Richmond Heights Historical Society Collection.)

Seen here in the 1950s is the intersection of Brentwood Boulevard and Clayton Road. Shortly after this photograph was taken, the vacant property in the foreground became the predecessor to the current Galleria Shopping Center, the Westroads Shopping Center. (Courtesy of the Richmond Heights Historical Society Collection.)

While many of these buildings remain, the businesses have changed, the road has widened, and on-street parking is no longer allowed. This 1959 view looks south from Clayton Road along Big Bend Boulevard. Today, Castelli's Tuxedo Rentals has been replaced by Waldbart's Florist, and farther south on the right side of the street, the Richmond Theatre is now Mesa Cycles. On the left side of Big Bend, the Turnpike Restaurant is partially visible and behind it stands National Food Store. A medical building has since replaced the restaurant, and the grocery store is now an Office Depot. (Courtesy of the Richmond Heights Historical Society Collection.)

This 1962 aerial view looks south from Clayton Road almost to where it intersects with Brentwood Boulevard on the right. To the left of Tropicana Bowling Lanes are the Sheridan Hills and Lavinia Gardens neighborhoods. To the right of the bowling alley is Francis Place. These communities were reduced drastically in the 1970s when Interstate 170 was built. More of Sheridan Hills and Lavinia Gardens is set to be taken when the Missouri Department of Transportation widens Interstate 40/64 in 2007–2008. (Courtesy of the Richmond Heights Historical Society Collection.)

Original Richmond Heights Historical Society board members pictured in 1984 are, from left to right, Joellen McDonald, Robert James, Edna Taylor, Evelyn Grant, Alice Sargent, Lorraine Johnson, and Alice Provaznik. Missing from the photograph are Nelson Clark, Don Dill, and Ken Williamson.

These two photographs are part of the Richmond Heights Historical Society Collection, but there is no information available about either one. The family portrait was originally on a glass plate. The automobile photograph shows what might be a Dort convention in either 1916 or 1917. Neither the building in the background nor the men in the image have been identified, and it is not understood why black cats decorate the automobile. Information about either of these photographs will be gratefully received.

BIBLIOGRAPHY

City of Richmond Heights. Business Directory, 7th Anniversary Edition. Self-published, 1988.

City of Richmond Heights. City of Richmond Heights: 50th anniversary souvenir booklet. Self-published, 1963.

City of Richmond Heights. "Nominate Your Neighbor" 2006–2007 municipal calendar. Self-published, 2006.

Hannon, Robert E., ed. St. Louis: Its Neighborhoods and Neighbors, Landmarks and Milestones. St. Louis: St. Louis Regional Commerce and Growth Association, 1986.

Heffley, Floyd S. "Historical Development of the Elementary Schools of the Maplewood-Richmond Heights School District, 1854–1944." Master's thesis, Saint Louis University, 1944.

Hillard, Robert. "Know Your County: Richmond Heights." St. Louis Star-Times. February 12, 1946.

http://www.census.gov

Leonard, John W., ed. The Book of St. Louisans: A Biographical Dictionary of Leading Living Men of the City of St. Louis. St. Louis: The St. Louis Republic, 1906.

Mahoney, Elizabeth. "Richmond Heights, Missouri." May 10, 1965.

"Richmond Heights." MS Maplewood-Richmond Heights High School, 1939.

O'Connor, Rev. P. J. History of Cheltenham and St. James Parish. St. Louis: St. James the Greater, 1937.

Primm, James Neal. Lion of the Valley: St. Louis, Missouri, 1764–1980. St. Louis: Missouri Historical Society Press, 1981.

Richmond Heights City and Business Directory. Self-published, 1930.

Richmond Heights Historical Society. "Down Memory Lane." Unpublished booklet. Richmond Heights, MO: 1988.

Saint Louis County Department of Parks and Recreation. The Past in Our Presence: Historic Buildings in St. Louis County. Self-published, 1996.

Terry, Dickson. "Richmond Heights in a Jubilee Mood." St. Louis Post Dispatch.

Young, Andrew D. Streets and Streetcars of St. Louis: A Sentimental Journey. St. Louis: Archway Publishing, 2002.

Wayman, Norbury. History of St. Louis Neighborhoods: Oakland and Clifton. St. Louis: St. Louis Community Development Agency, 1978.

Visit us at
arcadiapublishing.com